How to write an Amazon book that SELLS*

by

David Kessler

by someone who HAS... MANY TIMES !

ISBN 978-1519453709

Copyright © 2015 David Kessler

The right of David Kessler to be identified as the Author of this Work have been asserted by him in accordance with the Copyright, Designs and Patents Act 1988.

All rights reserved. No part of this publication may be reproduced, stored in a retrieval system, or transmitted, in any form or by any means, electronic, mechanical, photocopying, recording or otherwise, without the prior permission of the publisher.

Table of Contents

Other giveaways, cover reveals, guest posts, interviews, blog tours, etc.

A final word

Introduction

We live in exciting times. New technology. New ideas. New everything!

There once was a time when, if you wanted to get a book published you had to go to one of maybe two dozen publishers. Then the situation got worse and the publishers merged, bought each other out and "consolidated." That meant instead of being able to go to any of a couple of dozen publishers, you could now only go to maybe seven or eight.

Worse still you could no longer go to them directly. You had to go through an agent. And worse still, the agents were very picky and if you couldn't convince them that you were worth their effort, then you couldn't get past the gatekeepers and could never get your work onto the desk of an editor at a publishing house.

I remember, with one of my books, writing to a batch of some thirty agents, before I found four who were ready to even read it. (Please note: with most of these agents, you had to write a query letter first.) And one of those four even sent me another letter a few days later saying DON'T send the manuscript. Apparently, two different readers at the agency had conflicting opinions – and the left hand didn't know what the right hand was doing!

Or maybe just the whole process was completely random anyway – and in no way related to the actual quality of the book. Certainly the book could not have been *complete* rubbish, because another agent represented me and eventually – after some time I might add – managed go get me a two book deal with Hodder Headline.

And the book in question became my first published book: a legal thriller called *A Fool for a Client* that was reviewed by Susanna Yager in the *Sunday* Telegraph. Her review contained the immortal line: "The author has thought up the most ingenious method of committing murder that I have come across in a long time."

But now the rules have changed again because we now have eBooks – both on the Kindle platform and on the many other eBook platforms including tablets and smartphones. And remember that in 2014 alone, *one BILLION smart phones were sold!*

That's quite SOME audience to reach out to.

Of course, self-publishing, "subsidy publishing" and "vanity publishing" had been around for donkey's years before that. **But subsidy publishing was, is and will always remain a scam to bilk writers of their money.**

Self-publishing, on the other hand, using a low cost *printing* (not "subsidy publishing") company (e.g. in China or India) is *not* a scam. But it is still usually a way to lose money. It is very hard to get the high street bookshops to carry your books. And in the meantime, you will have spent a lot of money on making the plates, printing a batch of copies, etc.

But electronic publishing, and to some extent Print on Demand (in conjunction with online markets such as Amazon) have created a whole new ball game!

That's the **good** news.

So what's the **bad** news?

The bad news is that the whole world and his brother are doing it! Everyone thinks he/she is a writer. Sure you can now get your work out there, without having to hand over your life savings to some dodgy "subsidy publisher." But so can everyone else. So you're facing stiff competition.

But what can you do about that?

The answer is two-fold. Firstly you can write a book that people actually want to *read*. Then after that you can do all the right things to *sell* it! That means, promote it, get it noticed and get people talking about it and buying it.

In fact there's more to it than that, because to make money selling Kindle books – unless you happen to strike it lucky – you must write a *lot* of books. That means not being lazy and having lots of ideas.

I have had many books published both under my own name and under a whole slew of pen-names. I have been published by traditional print publishers, such as Hodder Headline, HarperCollins and Greenzone. But I have also published far more books myself for the Kindle and other eBook platforms. What's more I have written books in many different genres: thrillers, historical, science fiction, children's *and even chick-lit!*

Indeed one of the reasons I branched out into self-publishing – *despite being published by several major print publishers* – is because my publishers wanted to cramp my style and limit me to particular genres, instead of letting me broaden my repertoire.

This does not mean that you *must* write books in more than one genre. You are perfectly free to stick to one genre and do it well. But the important thing is that you must be ready to be hard-working and prolific. If you can manage that – if you can resist the distractions of the internet, and the desire to "surf", I can guide you through the process of writing good books, starting with the basics and working up to the finer details and then the process of selling your books.

So you really want to be a successful author of eBooks for the Kindle and other platforms? Read on...

Chapter 1 – How to get *ideas*

When you tell other people that you write novels or fiction or stories or thrillers or romance, the first question you hear is: "from where do you get your ideas?"

Like "the check is in the mail," it is a phrase that should be put on a plaque and hung on the wall. Most writers – being good with words after all – will make some half-hearted effort to answer the question. But it does get tiresome after a while.

Part of the problem is that even though writers are good with words and good at understanding the psychology of other people – including our characters. We are not so good at understanding our own thought processes. Unless we are also avid keepers of diaries, we have, in many cases, only the most rudimentary idea of where our story ideas came from. Even if we can remember where we got the idea for the BIG STORY, what about that little episode in the middle? That eccentric character who popped in for a walk on part. That house with the strange architecture? That landscape that we described so well?

Part of the problem is that even if you, the writer, can answer the question, the people who asked it haven't really got the patience to listen. What they want is a sound-byte, not a lecture. But the trouble is, there *is* no easy answer. No sound byte can encapsulate either the generic answer of where do author's ideas come from or the specific question with regard to a particular book.

One generic answer that one sometimes hears is that it starts with the hypothetical thought: wouldn't it be interesting if...

That's really a good answer as far as it goes, but where do all these *iffs* come from?

You see? We're back too Square One.

To find the answer, we're going to have to dig a little deeper.

Your Personal Experience

The first source of good ideas is, of course, your own personal experience. This can be many things. And you don't have to have been a former special forces soldier or a test pilot, to have interesting experiences that can inspire stories. For example, even a simple argument with your neighbor that gets out of hand could give rise to the speculation: *what if I'd killed him?*

All of a sudden you now have the basis for a story about an ordinary man or woman who finds themselves charged with murder and gets drawn into the legal system, or even the prison system. At least, you have the *beginning* of a story. You may have to bolster your initial idle speculation. You may have to research how the legal system deals with such cases. And you may have to speculate further on the mindset of the ordinary person, turned killer. But for now, at least, you have the starting point for a story.

In practice this breaks down into many sub-categories, covering not only things that have happened to you, but also events affecting family and friends.

Or let's take another example. Let's say that you are employed in a full-time job. You don't have tenure, or contractual job security, but you are doing your job well and the economy is sound, with no sign of recession on the horizon. Then, one day – out of the blue – your boss calls you into his office and tells you that the company is downsizing and you are being laid off.

Well of course, your initial reaction is a mixture of anger and confusion. First of all you had no idea that the company was in trouble. Work days appeared to be as busy as usual. There were no quiet days. No lost or canceled contracts. There hasn't been a stock market collapse or a major financial crisis. The economy appears to be holding up and you have never given your boss a reason to say a bad word about you.

Why? Your mind shrieks.

And it gets worse. Because then you start thinking about your colleagues. Some of them are a lot less efficient or competent than you. Why are *you* being let go and not them? Indeed if the company is downsizing then why are *you* the only one who has been handed a pink slip?

As these thoughts of frustration build up in your mind, festering into paranoia, you speculate that there must be more to it. Something sinister. Maybe a colleague you thought you could trust stabbed you in the back. Or maybe the boss has been fiddling the company tax returns and he was afraid that you'd be the smart employee who might figure it out and blow the whistle? Or maybe he was having an affair with a major customer's wife and you caught them in an almost-intimate moment.

You go home. You open a can of Bud and you think about it.

Under the sedentary and calming influence of your spouse, your anger is assuaged and you abandon these feelings of paranoia. You realize that it was more likely exactly what your boss said: a case of downsizing in the face of stagnant markets and foreign competition. You're still bitter and angry, but what can you do? There's not much you *can* do really except pick yourself up out of the gutter and find a new job.

But in the meantime something has happened. Well two things actually.

The first is that without even realizing it you have started to develop an idea for a story. It may not have enough detail to flesh out a full-length novel. But it certainly has enough to fill a short story or to *develop* into a complete novel by the addition of further material.

The bad news is that in your rejoicing, you have put the idea aside. Now that you have found that new job and come to realize that you were just the unlucky victim of "corporate downsizing," you have abandoned all those thoughts of intrigue and financial/sexual shenanigans. In other words, like a fleeting dream that seemed so vivid in those few seconds after you first woke up, the story has all but gone.

But wait a minute… *what if it hasn't?* What if instead of forgetting it, you still remember some of the details of your paranoid fantasy? What if you wrote some of it down? Maybe you were planning to write a letter of complaint to the DOJ or the FBI. Or maybe you were planning on blogging about it and letting all the shareholders know what you suspected. Maybe you were planning an appeal to a labor tribunal. Whatever the reason, let's say that some of the ideas have been preserved either in your head or on paper.

Now maybe a new thought has entered your head? *What if I take these ideas and turn them into a thriller?*

You have just taken the first step on the long and lonely road to becoming a writer.

Now I am not saying that you should abandon the new-found security of the job you've just started and write full-time in the hope of achieving instant publication. Apart from anything else, the local Benefits Agency might have something to say if you don't appear to be looking for a job or if you aren't available for full-time employment.

But if you can manage to muster the self-discipline to put in an hour in the evening, when you come home dog-tired and a few hours at the weekend when the kids are nagging you for attention, then you could be on the way to becoming a writer.

That, however, comes later. We're still looking at the role of personal experience in getting ideas for stories. Your place of work can be an interesting starting point. Even if the place where you work is dull, even if the work you do is boring, it is still possible to imagine an interesting event springing out of a boring place. Very often the more boring the work environment, the more likely you are to daydream and those daydreams can also be fuel for a good story. The trick is to hang on them: write them down. Then when you have gathered enough material for a story, you will find — quite possibly to your own surprise — that the material is leaping off the page at you and begging you to write it.

Personal experience can of course mean different things to different people. It can cover anything from the trivial, to the serious. Let me give a couple of examples based on my own experience.

My mother died of cancer when I was in my mid-teens. A couple of years later, the provisional IRA (and Irish nationalist organization) planted a bomb under a car outside the home of businessman Sir Hugh Fraser. For whom the bomb was intended is not clear, as the young Caroline Kennedy was staying at the house at the time, and she was known to use the car. In the event, what happened was that a man was walking his dog in the morning and the dog went under the car, pulled out the bomb and brought it to the man, whereupon it exploded, killing the man. Now it just so happens that the man in question was one of Britain's leading cancer specialists.

When I heard about the incident in the news, I had a very interesting thought: in killing this *one* man and destroying forever his brain, his skill and his knowledge, the terrorists had not only killed an individual, but had also indirectly killed many others whom that man – a leading cancer specialist – could have saved. And of course, as I mentioned, my mother had died of cancer only two years before that. Not that my mother was one of those he could have saved. But nevertheless I wondered how some one would feel if they watched their mother, or any close relative, wasting away of cancer, knowing — or at least believing — that their loved one could have been saved had it not been for the terrorist act that murdered the cancer specialist who might have saved them.

This, I realized, might give rise to a desire for revenge, one of the most compelling motives in life… and in literature!

At the more trivial level, I once noticed a warning on an insecticide canister that it contained pyrethrum, a well-known nerve poison. It stated in bold letters that the antidote to pyrethrum was atropine. But I already knew from another source that atropine is itself a poison (also known as belladonna and extracted from the Deadly Nightshade plant).

Out of this collection of "experiences" came an interesting speculative thought: what if some one tricks another person into

14

believing that he has been poisoned with a large dose of pyrethrum so that the doctors give the "victim" a fatal dose of atropine, intending it to combat the pyrethrum?

Of course this raw idea is full of holes that need to be plugged. How does one make sure that the doctors give the patient a large enough does of atropine to kill him? How does one make sure that they act in haste? Would they not perform tests in order to find out if the "patient" has really imbibed such a large dose of pyrethrum? How quickly does pyrethrum act when ingested orally (as opposed to though the skin)?

All of these questions need to be answered and resolved using another part of the writer's toolkit: *research*. In a worst-case scenario, if some of the problems prove to be insurmountable, one can always invoke literary license. (Which I did – in *spades*!)

But the important thing, as far as getting ideas is concerned, is that as soon as I saw that label on the insecticide canister, I had an idea for an element of a story. What I did with that thought demonstrates the classic "what if...?" approach that is the key to getting story ideas. I took a basic reality and created an alternative to it. This is the key to getting story ideas. You ask "what if..." and it doesn't matter what the rest of the sentence was. Once the writer speculates on some one doing something involving murder, theft, espionage, crime, intrigue... *conflict*... that is the starting point of a story.

In fact the story that utilized that idea above about the poison was to undergo much evolution before it ended up in print. I used the idea first in a short story which basically described the build-up to the killing, followed by the killing itself which also revealed the motive. The story was not bad, although it is not something I would be proud to share with the world today. Later I wove the single strand of that basic premise, together with the cancer "motive" above, into the fabric of a much more elaborate story that I wrote as a full-length book. Originally titled *What Happened Where?* It went on to become *A Fool for a Client*, my first published thriller.

You'll note that in that long string of abstract nouns I used above for possible themes of a story, the one I ended up with was *conflict*. This

15

is very important because it summarizes all the others. Conflict is the life-blood of almost all works of fiction. I say "almost" because there are also "mood pieces" in short story format in which there is no conflict, only contemplation. But these pieces are a minority of fiction writers' output and once you get up to a full-length novel (or a screenplay for that matter) you are dealing in conflict as the driving force behind the characters in your story. In essence, the reason you have a story is because at least one of your characters wants to do something and someone or some*thing* stands in their way!

In mysteries suspense novels and thrillers, this conflict usually centers around such things as crime or war. In romance, chick-lit and erotica, it is unrequited love – or love rivalry. In war stories and epic tales it might be a conflict between nations, or even planets. But not all of these things are particularly common in the average person's life. Love triangles mainly, but how many people get involved in murder? How many are soldiers?

So from *where else* might the aspiring author get ideas?

The News

Well one obvious answer is the news. We are bombarded with news all the time, some of it serious, much of it trivial. But within it there is plenty of material to fuel the creative urges of an army of aspiring writers. Remember what I said before about the IRA bomb that killed the cancer specialist a couple of years after my mother died of cancer? My mother's death was a personal tragedy that affected me and my family. But the murder of the cancer specialist was a news event that captured my attention because of the way it linked up with my personal experience.

You will find stories to give you ideas at all levels or journalism – from the financial shenanigans exposed by the liberal broadsheets to the incompetence of government exposed by the right-wing broadsheets, to the "human interest" stories in the tabloids and the National Enquirer.

Another source of information is television news. And these days, we've also got the internet.

Even *old* news can be the jumping off point for a story. Once, while visiting the house of a friend of a friend in Israel, I made a chance remark about Kew Gardens in London. My host, an American psychology student in her early twenties, asked me if I was talking about "Kitty Genovese." At the time, I didn't have a clue who Kitty Genovese was. But I soon found out.

She was talking about Kew Gardens in New York city – and specifically the infamous murder of the aforesaid Kitty Genovese. According to the accounts that were circulated in the press at the time (although they have since been called into question), the murderous knife attack on Kitty Genovese was not only brutal, but also a slow, drawn-out affair, lasting about half an hour. While the attack was in progress, over a dozen people allegedly came to the windows of nearby apartments, overlooking the scene of the incident, alerted by Kitty's screams. The reports claimed that these onlookers witnessed the attack but supposedly did nothing to help the victim. Pop-psychology analysis claimed that this was not due to cowardice, because the witnesses didn't even phone the police – which would have entailed no risk. Nor yet was it mere indifference – because although they didn't intervene or call the police, they stood their watching the attack, rather than just going away and forget about it.

The case had become something of a landmark study in the psychology of bystanders behavior and for that reason was well-known to the student. She hurriedly thumbed through one of her textbooks and handed me a chapter or section about the case and the psychological research that was carried out in its aftermath.

The research involved a now-classic experiment that established that when a person is alone in a room and hears a person scream, they are apt to go and investigate, to find out what is going on and if they can help. But if some one else is in the room with them (the experimenter's assistant) and does not appear to react to the scream, then they too tend not to react. Sometimes they show surprise or alarm. But if the other person remains apparently indifferent then they tend to take no action.

This is partly due to embarrassment and partly due to the fact that they reassure themselves that if the other person seems unperturbed then "it was probably just my imagination." That is believed by many to be what happened in the case of Kitty Genovese. The eyewitnesses assumed that the attack in the distance could not be all that serious, because no one else was interfering or taking action. Alternatively, they may also have assumed that some one else would already have phoned the police and therefore there was no need for them to do likewise.

In fact some of the assumptions about what actually happened in Kitty Genovese case were wrong – the results of journalistic hyperbole by one particular journalist. But I didn't know that at the time and in any case, for my creative purposes, it was irrelevant.

My interest in the case came from a completely different angle. *What*, I speculated, wearing my writer's hat, if one solitary individual *had indeed* gone to her aid? And what if in order to confront the armed attacker, our "Good Samaritan" had grabbed some object, like say a broken stick of furniture or the fallen branch of a tree, with which to fend off the attacker? And what if at precisely that point the police arrived? And what if the attacker saw the police before they saw him and simply ran away? Stay with me...

And what if the police saw the "Good Samaritan" who had just come to the victim's rescue standing over the victim – still in the grip of adrenaline and tension – with his improvised "weapon" and assumed that he was the attacker? And what if one of those cops shot him (if the story was set in the United States) or whacked him on the head with a baton (if it was set in Britain)? In other words, what if the brave man who had gone to the aid of the victim ended up dead or in a coma, through the actions of an over-zealous cop.

Those speculations had already taken me quite far. But there was a lot further still to go. For example what if the cop who acted so precipitately was not some jaded old-timer, but rather a young, inexperienced "rookie" who still had the fire of youthful ideals burning in his belly? And what if the discovery that he had killed or injured not merely the "wrong" man, but actually a good and courageous man, left the young cop emotionally scarred or psychologically shattered?

But wait! There's more. For what if, alternatively, the man who had gone to the woman's aid actually *had* dropped the stick or branch when he saw the police? And then – yes, our storyline is really coming along nicely now – what if the cynical older *partner* of the young idealistic cop looks down at the victim lying there and then looks up at the man who until a moment ago was holding a blunt object which in the darkness looks like it *could* have been the attack weapon which has left the woman bleeding and on the verge of death? So, in a fit of rage, the older cop hits the man whom he believes to be the attacker, out of a sense of revenge, even though the man is obviously no threat to them at that stage, regardless of what had come before?

Now, our young rookie has a moral dilemma. Should he cover for his partner by lying for him? Even after it becomes clear that his partner hit the wrong man? Or should his sympathy with the innocent man prompt him to tell the truth? As you can see, these "what if" questions have taken us along way. But if we carry on running with the ball, they can take us yet further still, as you will see below.

What is already clear however is that even something as innocuous as a chapter or passage in a psychology book – or indeed any non-fiction publication – can provide food for the writer's creative imagination. All it takes is a questioning mind to latch on to the potential in the chapter or passage and to keep asking the questions that naturally occur to a creative mind.

To give another – briefer – example of this mental process: I read an article about genetic engineering and how one could splice the gene sequence for the "active ingredient" of one plant into another. For example the genetic sequence for a toxic substance that protects a plant from pests could be spliced into another so that the new genetically modified plant will have the same pest resistance as the plant that it borrowed the DNA from. While reading the article, I had the idea that one could splice the active ingredient of the coca plant – the genes that produce cocaine – into a plant used in the production of perfume and thus create an addictive perfume. While the idea may not be completely scientific, it was sufficiently plausible for me to use in a book.

These are examples of how obscure academic texts or popular expositions of new ideas in science can give rise to a story, or at least a major *element* of the story. But at the other extreme, and perhaps more obviously, there are the famous cases, the *causes celebres*, that hit the front pages of our newspapers. These are a more obvious source of story ideas.

One of the real life cases that exercised a powerful influence on me was the Colin Stagg case. Colin Stagg was accused of the murder of a young woman called Rachel Nickell on Wimbledon Common. He was initially arrested and released, but the police remained interested in him and conducted a honey-trap operation to try to get evidence against him. Although he never confessed, the police thought that the had accumulated enough evidence to build a case against him and accordingly they re-arrested him and charged him. But the judge – who was normally sympathetic to the police, and by no means a bleeding heart liberal – thought otherwise. He threw out much of the so-called evidence as being prejudicial and lacking probative value, bringing about the collapse of the prosecution case before it was ever presented to he jury.

But this – paradoxically – made things even worse for the suspect Colin Stagg. For it led t a widespread perception of him as a guilty man who had beaten the rap. This perception was enhanced by police leaks and one-sided journalism from some of the newspapers.

I became interested in the case precisely because the press reports were almost invariably hostile to Stagg. When I read between the lines, I noticed a lot of holes in the case against him. It seemed to me that both the police and the more right-wing newspapers were mountains our of molehills. This led me to research the case in some detail and culminated in by co-writing a book about the case with Colin Stagg, putting to the reader the case for the defense.

However, before that, I considered the case as a possible source of ideas for a work cf fiction. One aspect of the case involved an undercover policewoman calling herself Lizzie James, who befriended Stagg. She exchanged letters with him, spoke to him on the phone and had four meetings with him in an unsuccessful effort to get him to confess. Nevertheless, the police thought that she had gathered enough from him by way of statements about the crime to charge him with murder. He maintained that he based his knowledge of the crime on local gossip (that turned out to have been started by a talkative coroner's assistant) and what he gleaned from three days of interrogation by the police.

I was interested in many aspects of the real case, but thinking about it as fodder for a work of fiction, I let my imagination run riot. What if the undercover police woman in that case was killed a few years later in the same way as the original victim in the earlier case? What if the suspect whom she once tried to entrap has been following her? What if that suspect sees her being attacked and goes to her aid? Here we see how an idea from one source can neatly dovetail into an idea from another source.

I am not the first writer to be inspired by news events. Nor will I surely be the last. Robert Ludlum's brilliant thriller *The Chancellor Manuscript* was based on the premise that a group of high-minded shaker-movers, calling themselves "Inver Brass", killed former FBI chief J Edgar Hoover and got their hands on the secret files that he had been using to blackmail presidents, senators, congressman, businessmen and many others. But problems arise when a corrupt member of Inver Brass, unknown to the others, starts using the information in the files to blackmail some of those same people in order to further his own nefarious agenda,.

Ludlum's starting point was almost certainly the news reports after Hoover's death that revealed the *existence* of those files: it wasn't something he just made up. Since then, it has emerged that while Hoover had the dirt on politician's and businessmen, the Italian-

American Mafia had the dirt on him, in the form of proof that he was a homosexual and a transvestite. This explains why Hoover refused to acknowledge the existence of organized crime until a mobster called Joe Valachi testified before Senator John L. McClellan's Permanent Subcommittee on Investigations, revealing the existence of "Cosa Nostra" in such detail that Hoover could no longer deny it. The revelations about Hoover's homosexuality along with the Mafia blackmail that resulted from it, offer scope for many more thrillers, no doubt some yet to be written.

Another book by Ludlum, *Trevayne*, was a thriller about senate investigations into military expenditure and was almost certainly inspired by some of the scandals of the Nixon administration in the early 1970s. Watergate was the most famous of those scandals but there were others, leading up to Watergate, some involving big business and the so-called "military-industrial complex."

Agatha Christie's mystery *Murder on the Orient Express*, used as its starting point the kidnap and murder of the baby of Charles Lindbergh, the pilot who is quite wrongly thought to have been the first man to fly across the Atlantic Ocean. The story wasn't about the murder of the baby but rather about the aftermath: how certain people behaved as a *result* of the murder.

The Death of Me Yet by Whit Masterton was based on the revelation that the Russian KGB had a mock-up American small town where they trained intelligence operatives to pose as American citizens. *The Big Byte* by Peter J Ognibene combined financial computer crime and religious cults. Presumably drawing on events in the news in 1980s America. The TV series *The Fugitive*, although not actually a book, was based on the criminal conviction of Dr Sam Shepherd for the murder of his wife, a case that culminated in a lengthy appeals process, a re-trial, an acquittal and a civil lawsuit.

All of those above example show how events that feature in the news can find their way into thrillers and mystery novels, not necessarily unadulterated, but in a form that suits the creative urges of the writer and doesn't merely "fictionalize" a well-known real event. We can be sure that even now people are writing war and spy thrillers about western military action in Serbia and Kosovo, about the murder of a pretty TV personality, about road rage attacks like the one committed by professional criminal Kenneth Noye and murders disguised as road rage attacks, like the one in which a young woman killed her fiancé, apparently in the heat of an argument.

I have a scrapbook of old news clippings that includes reports about several road-rage drivers, a student who was expelled for cheating on questionable evidence, a policeman who almost certainly sexually harassed a policewoman and got away with it and a convicted rapist who couldn't be tried for another rape on a minor because the judge ruled that after the first trial he couldn't get a fair trial on the additional charge. It also has stories about a suspected Israeli Mole at the White House, a report about a teenage girl who was suspended from school for writing letters complaining about absenteeism by teachers and an article about alleged Masonic influence in the police and judiciary.

These sort of stories can be used in stories in a number of ways. One is wish-fulfillment: i.e. writing a story in which the villains gets their comeuppance. Another is investigative: a story describing how the villain was caught. Yet another might be a story based on the premise that the authorities got the wrong man. Each of these involves a slightly different approach, but all are equally valid *points of departure* from the original story.

Other people's books

You'll note that I used, just now, a phrase that I haven't used so far: "Points of Departure." What does this phrase mean? Basically just what it sounds like. The point at which an invented story departs from some real event whether of a personal nature or something that one heard about in the news.

But one can also use point of departure in another way, as branches leading off from some one else's story. *But hold it*, you may say, *using some one else story?* Isn't that **plagiarism?** Well the answer is it depends on how you do it.

First of all it is important to distinguish between plagiarism, which is a moral issue, and copyright infringement, which is a legal one. This book does not purport to offer legal advice but in general it may be said that copying significant or substantial portions of another persons work without permission, whether it be blocks of text or an entire story-line in different words is or could be viewed as copyright infringement.

But what if it is more subtle than that? For example what if a composer and lyricist write a musical play inspired by Shakespeare's *Romeo and Juliet* but change the setting from Verona in Italy to New York in the 1950s? And change the antagonists from two feuding families to the street gangs? (Nowadays if would be the Crips and the Bloods in Los Angeles.)

Or what if a writer writes a story from the point of view of a *cat* inspired by a similar story by another, lesser known, writer? That is clearly not copyright infringement. But is it plagiarism?

Plagiarism is the use or appropriation of another person's words or *ideas* without giving credit. Even a brief quote from some one else without giving credit (or anonymous credit if the author is unknown) is plagiarism. Likewise paraphrasing some one else's ideas and presenting them as ones own original ideas is plagiarism. Of course if one conceives an idea truly independently of another one can offer it up as ones own. If one later discovers the similarity with some one else's ideas, one can always politely acknowledge the earlier work while asserting the originality of ones own.

But aside from the escape clause of giving credit to the original author, it is also possible to use another author's work in a way that is so oblique as to remove the need for giving credit. Let me give you and example.

I read a book many years ago in which a professional hit-man kills some one and then takes his gold pen, wallet and watch to make it look like a mugging. Shortly after that, he drives through an inner city ghetto and throws the items out of the window, knowing that the goods will be seized by whoever finds them and that accordingly the items are unlikely to turn up in the hands of the police. And even if they do, the original killing will still look like a mugging and the person in possession of the goods will get the blame.

As I read that passage, I had this idle thought: what if the stolen items do indeed turn up in such a context as to make it clear that they were *not* stolen in a mugging? Would this not prompt the police to re-investigate the original murder? At that point – or rather some time later – my mind went into passing gear, speculating on further scenarios. What if, in the meantime, the cops have arrested a man for the original murder – or even secured a guilty verdict – and now the DA has to reconsider his/her position?

Or what if instead of being thrown out of a car, the valuable items are thrown into a river or canal? What if another body is found floating on the river or canal which *prompts* the police to dredge or search that part of the river or canal? What if the police find a watch while dredging or diving in search of a murder weapon from this second *murder*? What if the watch in question is a Rolex *that can be identified by its serial number*? What if the two murders are linked? What if the act of finding the watch forces the police teams investigating the separate murders to pool their efforts?

This mass of idle speculations found its way into *The Other Victim,* my second book, originally titled *The Scent of Death.* I cannot for the life of me remember the title or author of the work that gave rise to these speculations and I doubt that the author would even recognize any trace of his own work if he read *The Other Victim.* Nevertheless, I can confide in the reader that certain aspects of that other book prompted my speculations. And that, in essence is a **point of departure**.

There are endless ways in which some one else's ideas can branch off into new and original ways of ones own. A story about a terrorist outrage can leave you thinking about one of the victims. What is *their* story? A legal thriller focusing on a lawyer can lead to the reader thinking about the life and loves and career problems of a juror. A spy thriller featuring fast cars can rise to thoughts about industrial espionage in the automobile design and manufacture industry.

25

In William Goldman's *Marathon Man* there are several examples of how other people's stories can branch off from the main one without being developed into full length themes by the author. After a road rage scene culminating in a collision between a car and an oil tanker vehicle, causing a huge explosion, Goldman tells the reader briefly how the explosion launched the career of a photographer nearby who happened to get a photograph of the tragedy and a man who finally managed to get it together with a waitress that he'd been "hitting on" for some time – because of the psychological impact of the tragedy.

All this is just crying out for some one to lift those characters (or people like them) and follow up on their stories... and hope that William Goldman doesn't sue!

Overheard conversations

It's happened to all of us. You've been sitting in a bar or café, there is a lull in the conversation with your friends and you catch a snippet of some one else's conversation at a neighboring table.

Or perhaps, if you're a loner like me (and many writer's are) you were in the bar or café alone, maybe making notes for your next book, when some people sat at the table next to you and you were treated to an entire conversation, not just a brief snippet.

Then again, maybe you were on a bus or train and you had the benefit of a long journey to overhear a conversation between two people about their mutual friend.

Whichever of these it was, if you have the creative spirit in you then you would probably have been left thinking about those details and tried to flesh them out in your mind. You want to know the rest: the beginning that you missed; the end that you never heard because they got off the bus or because *you* had to.

You are thinking like a writer, because you know that in what you heard, there is the essence of a story. Maybe only a short story. Or maybe a key element of a full-length novel. Or maybe yet something different; a character profile of a major character *within* a story. But whatever it is, it is grist for your creative mill.

In my case it was lunch at a pub near the office where I worked as a technical writer. A young man and woman (both in their late twenties or early thirties) came and sat at the table next to mine. At first I read the book I had brought with me - I think it was about how to be a master criminal, or something like that. But as their conversation wafted towards me I soon realized that I was hearing something far more useful to me as a writer than anything I could read in the book I had brought with me.

It wasn't so much the conversation that fascinated as the *woman*. She was a fascinating character and — in my opinion — rather an obnoxious one. First of all she was neither specially attractive nor particularly ugly. Pretty much in-between, so it clearly wasn't her looks that were affecting my judgment. What was also clear about her was that she was extremely *tough*. I don't mean physically. She was not a big woman, being neither muscular nor fat. She may have possessed some martial arts skills for all I knew, but their was nothing in her physique or posture to suggest it. But she was tough as nails on the inside. And I don't mean aggressive, I mean tough.

I'll give just two examples. At one point in the conversation the man said something that I didn't hear clearly. It was before the stage that I was actively listening to the conversation and it was the woman's reaction that made me start paying attention. She said in a quiet, dismissive tone: "I didn't ask you for your permission. One usually waits to be asked for permission before granting it." Her tone wasn't defensive nor was it aggressive. It was calculated to make the man feel small and by his sheepish reaction I got the impression that it succeeded. I found her tone and general demeanor rather irritating. But I was *fascinated* by it, and by *her*.

From then on I hung to every word she said, as did her male companion. She talked incessantly about this and that, while he made the occasional grant or asked a question when she paused. One of the incidents she mentioned was how she had recently slapped her brother when he used vulgar language in her presence. She gave a

27

graphic impression of how she did it, her hand swishing backward and forward in the air. When her companion asked how her brother reacted she replied: "Oh he said 'don't you do that to me' and ran away." From various things she said just before and just after that, I got the impression that her brother was a teenager.

Like I said, tough as nails.

I can't in all honesty say that I like her. But a writer doesn't have to like all his characters. He does however have to be fascinated by them.

On another occasion I heard one of my female work colleagues tell another that she resented the fact that her father was preparing his son, her younger brother, to run the family oil business in Nigeria simply because he was a man, even though she understood the business better than her brother. This is a theme that I kept in my mental scrap-book of "to be used" items. It later found its way into a short novel that I wrote under the pen-name Karen Dee – in the chick-lit genre, of all things!

Other sources of ideas

The sources of ideas above are a good starting point for the creative writer to think about. But the list is by no means exhaustive. Dreams – if you remember them – are an excellent starting point for stories.

My older sister once wrote a song based on a dream my younger sister told her about. All my younger sister could remember of the dream was a young woman standing at the top of a hill looking out to sea waiting for the return of a man from the wars. It was not clear from the visual imagery whether the man was her husband, lover, father or brother. And it was this question that hung over my younger sister when she woke up. Our older sister, who was the most musically talented member of the family (and also, perhaps, the most literarily gifted) wrote a song from the point of view of an omniscient voice speaking to the woman, telling her that he was gone forever. Although only a song, it actually encapsulated a whole story.

I once wrote the first draft of a novel based loosely on a dream However, the problem with dreams is that it is very hard to remember their details. One has to write them down when one is still tired, before waking up fully. What I usually find is that what seemed like a brilliant idea when I first woke up is really rather mundane and formulaic when I look at the notes afterwards. What makes dreams interesting is very often their vividness at the time rather than the underlying story that they tell.

Having said that, it has to be added that dreams remain a rich potential source of story ideas for some, if you know how to use them. I have heard that some authors who write about supernatural themes rely heavily on their dreams. According to Edward de Bono, one way to remember ones dreams is to eat chocolate the night before. That apparently produces vivid dreams. Indeed, according to Edward de Bono, the reason Sigmund Freud was such a great success was because the Viennese were voracious chocolate eaters – producing plenty of vivid dreams for him to analyze.

For the budding Hemmingways and Dylan Thomas's among you, dreams can also include drunken stupors. However, I don't advise you excessive consumption of alcohol in pursuit of literary inspiration. On the other hand, if it happens... *make the most of it!* After all, as in the case of the example above about getting laid off from ones job, what could be better than taking something bad in real life and turning it into something good on paper or the web?

Chapter 2 - How to Develop the Plot

We have seen so far, that it is possible to get ideas from a variety of sources. But getting ideas is only the first stage of the writers long and arduous journey. The next step is weaving these strands of ideas into the fabric of a story.

Combining the plots and story lines

I have compared the process of creating a full length book or screenplay to weaving separate strands together. But as in the rag trade one cannot just mix and match any old strands. The strands must *belong* together — they must *match* rather than *clash* — otherwise one gets a patchwork quilt instead of an elegant garment.

This means that one shouldn't force story ideas together arbitrarily: one should think about which ideas *naturally* belong together. For example, my thoughts about how the murder of the cancer specialist might give rise to a desire for revenge blended naturally with the idea of killing a person by making them think they've been poisoned with pyrethrum so that they're given toxic atropine as the antidote. But *why* do they go naturally together?

Well, let's think about it. We have an interesting and somewhat unusual *motive* to kill some one. Revenge, yes… but a very indirect and oblique motive for revenge. Therefore it is the sort of revenge that is liable to be sought by *some one with a very unusual mind* (a bit like this author in fact!). Then we have a somewhat unusual *method* of killing some one: a method that is likely to be thought of by… well… again, *some one with an unusual mind*. Who more likely to kill in this way than some one with an unlikely motive and an unusual frame of mind?

There are also other reasons why these strands fit so naturally together. It is such an unusual method of killing that, depending on how it is done, there's a chance that it may fall within a loophole in the law and the killer might get away with it. As the reader is quite likely to sympathize with the killer, it is quite sensible that we should choose a method of killing that gives our hero-killer has a sporting chance of getting away with it.

Let's take another example. As I hinted at above, the story about the public spirited citizen who goes to the aid of the woman being attacked can easily be combined with the thoughts arising out of the Colin Stagg case that I mentioned in Chapter 1. After all, if he followed the policewoman, out of curiosity for example, he would be in a good position to witness the attack. If he witnessed the attack, he might fear that he would be accused and this might prompt him to take action to stop the attack. Or, alternatively, he might agonize over whether to go to her aid or not.

The mere act of combining these two strands then gives rise to further questions. Like, what does the policeman do after he has killed the innocent man or put him in a coma? How does he handle his guilt? Does her go off and search for the real attacker/killer? Does he discover that it was the same attacker who killed the woman *in the original case?*

Or what if it was his *partner* who hit the man? And what if — like we considered before —the man who went to the woman's aid *had already dropped the stick*? Does our idealistic young cop snitch on his partner? And if he cannot bring himself to do so, then might he not start investigating the murder as an alternative way of expiating his own feelings of guilt?

But it is not *his* case to investigate. He is just a young uniformed patrolman, not a detective. And he's certainly not supposed to be going off like a loose cannon staging his own one-man investigation! So if he's found out before he solves the case, this would surely bring him into conflict with his own superiors. And if the dead woman was an undercover policewoman, perhaps he wouldn't even know it – until he stumbles across it further down the line. After all, in a police investigation, everything is done on a need to know basis. If he's not part of the investigation, then he doesn't need to know. But if he starts nosing around where sensitive matters are concerned, his superiors are going to be none-too-pleased when they find out!

Thus from a couple of simple strands, our story begins to grow.

Let's take another example: the story fragment about the murder made to look like a mugging, with the Rolex watch turning up in the river or canal when the police are looking for the murder weapon used in the second crime. Who are the two victims? Are the crimes related. It makes sense if they are, especially if we're talking about a canal, where there is very little current, rather than a river. After all, the killer may have disposed of the body in the same spot where her threw the watch in after the first murder He may be familiar with the area. It may be easily accessible to him. It may be suitably secluded and thus an idea spot to dispose of a watch… or a body.

But still, who are the victims and why did he kill them? Maybe we should go back to that idea about the addictive perfume. Maybe one of the victims is the person who *created* the addictive perfume by some method of genetic engineering. And maybe he did it for others who were *paying* him. If so, then he might have been killed to shut him up.

That's a perfectly good motive. In fact, perhaps they were both killed to shut them up. Maybe one of them is a young chemistry genius who was persuaded to do the work for some criminal gang and maybe the other is some one who finds out it and is about to blow the whistle.

Alternatively, maybe the second victim is *part of the conspiracy!* Maybe he got cold feet when he realized that things were getting out of hand.

But if so, then who killed him? It would have to be another member of the conspiracy: some one more ruthless. So we now have another character to think about. Is this new person the leader of the conspiracy or is he an up-and-coming deputy leader anxious to seize the moment and take over when he detects signs of weakness in his superior?

This is the process of story development. We start by asking the question "what if…" over and over again to get the strands of a story. We weave the strands together and then we ask more questions to clarify the details and highlight the problems. As we answer these questions, we build up our story until we have a beginning a middle and an end. If these parts are enough to form a novel, we *write* a novel. If not, we write a novella or a screenplay or a short story.

Finding an interesting angle

In sifting through our story material we sometimes find problems. Is it consistent? Does it make sense? Is this behavior natural? But very often we also find another: is it original? Has it been done before? Is it hackneyed? Does it give you that sense of *déjà vu*?

Let's take the idea before about the policeman hitting the innocent man with a baton and putting him in a coma. I offered two scenarios. In one, the young idealistic policeman hit the innocent man by mistake, misjudging the danger in the darkness. He was motivated not by malice or even anger, but simply by fear and inexperience. He may get into trouble with his superiors for what he did. But we, the readers, cannot really blame him morally. It is just an unfortunate accident caused by a combination of darkness and youthful inexperience.

Now let's take the other scenario. The other police patrolman — possibly a cynical older cop who has lost his ideals and is perhaps even a trifle corrupt — sees the woman lying there bleeding. The man who went to her aid has dropped the stick or whatever that he used to fend off the real attacker, so there is no possibility that he is a threat to the police, whatever came before. But the older cop sees the female victim lying there in a pool of blood. It is dark so he cannot see the nature of the injuries. He saw the man holding a blunt object that *could* have been the attack weapon and he assumes that this is the man who committed the attack. He realizes that whatever penalty the courts can impose upon this man, it will never be as great as the evil he has apparently done and so – in a burst of anger – he lashes out with his baton, hitting the man on the head.

Note the differences in the two scenarios. In the first, the *young* cop did not do something morally wrong. But he did make an error of judgment which hangs over him like a cloud, affecting his actions for the rest of the story. In the second scenario, the young cop has not done something morally wrong *himself*, but he faces a moral dilemma. The matter will almost certainly come before their superiors for review. Apart from anything else, the baton is not supposed to be used on a suspect's head. The normal target area is the back of the leg. A well-aimed blow to the tendon at the back of the knee can bring a suspect down without causing any injury.

But our young idealistic hero now stands at an ethical fork in the road. Should he tell the truth to his superiors? Or should he lie for his colleague and say that it *looked* for a split second as if the man was about to attack them. Remember that morally if not legally his colleague meant well — he was motivated by a sense of intense sympathy towards the victim of a vicious murder. Consider further that these are the people that the young rookie cop will have to work with in the future. If he gets a reputation as one who snitches on a colleague, how will that effect his work relations and his career? Also, consider the fact that nothing he says will actually help the innocent man who is now in hospital on a life support system. The police already know by now that this man was *not* the attacker but rather a passer-by who went to the aid of the woman who was being attacked. So there is no danger of the man being tried for a crime he didn't commit. And if the young cop testifies against his colleague, it won't improve the health or physical condition of the man in hospital.

On the other hand if he doesn't spill the beans he'll be depriving another man of *justice*. The innocent man who went to the woman's aid surely has the right to see the wrongdoer punished (even if he doesn't literally "see" it). And when our young hero joined the police force it was because he was motivated by the ideal that wrongdoers should be punished. Now that he knows that the victim of his colleague's over-zealousness was an innocent man – even a hero in his own right – how can our protagonist turn his back on the ideals that prompted him to join the police in the first place? Should he turn his back on his conviction that wrongdoers should be punished simply because the wrongdoer, on this occasion, is his own colleague?

As outside observers, in the comfort our own living rooms, most of us can say exactly what our hero *ought* to do: he *ought* to tell his superiors the truth and if that sinks his partner and makes his own position in the police somewhat more uncomfortable then so be it.

But there is a problem here. If the reader knows what the hero *ought* to do, then they also know what sooner or later he *will* do. Although our hero's dilemma is tough to some one looking at it on the inside, it is very clear-cut when viewed from the outside. There may be a few dissenters, but I think most people would say that the decent thing to do is tell his partner that he is *going* to spill the beans to their superiors, thus giving his partner the chance to come clean himself. But if his partner doesn't do so, then our hero must by way of moral duty tell his superiors what really happened.

But supposing – just supposing – we make the young policeman's moral dilemma even *more* difficult? What if we combine the two scenarios above by making it *the young rookie cop* who strikes the blow that puts "Good Samaritan" in hospital, but that he does so *not as a misjudgment of the danger but rather for the reasons that we previously attributed to his partner*? That is, the "Good Samaritan" drops the branch or stick and the young rookie cop – in a fit of anger and sympathy for the woman victim, lying there in a pool of blood – lashes out at the man he thinks did it?

Now it's not so easy for him to tell the truth about what happened after he finds out that the man is innocent, is it? Because it is not his partner who did wrong, but he himself! If he comes clean now, and tells the truth, he'll effectively be spilling the beans on himself. And the effect of that would be that he is not only sinking his own career but even *exposing himself to the danger of criminal prosecution!*

But now, let's make it even *harder* for him! What if his partner complicates matters by going out on a limb *and lies for him*, saying that it looked as if the man was about to hit him with the stick? This adds yet another layer of complication to the situation. Because if he comes clean after this*, he'd not only sinking his own career but also dragging his partner down with him!* And to drag his partner down is bad enough, but drag him down after his partner **stuck his neck out for him** would be even worse. This greatly amplifies his dilemma.

35

As you can see, what starts off as a simple problem can become a lot more complicated. The saying "Oh what a tangled web we weave when first we practice to deceive," has endless variations and applications in literature. It is up to the writer to find ways of putting the old wine into a new bottle.

Or let's try a completely different genre: romance!

An emotionally-repressed older man gets into a relationship with a younger woman. How does it happen? Maybe they meet by chance in a park. Maybe she has a kid from an earlier relationship? And why are they attracted to each other? Maybe the kid brings them together? The man is... some sort of engineer. And the kid is a boy. And boys love gadgets. And the engineer is good at making gadgets. So the boy takes a shine to the engineer as a sort of father figure. And the woman sees this and so she warms to him too – sort of on the lines of: *if-my-boy-likes-him-then-he-must-be-all-right.*

Now there are all sorts of ways that this could go. If one wanted to take it in a sinister direction, one could give the man some deep dark secret. But what if we want to take it in the romantic direction. And what is the essence of romance? Boy meets girl. Boy loses girl. Boy gets girl.

Okay, but how does he lose the girl? Maybe there's an age difference? But that doesn't work, does it? After all, the age difference was there from the beginning. Well maybe the age difference manifests itself at a crucial moment, when the man lets her down. Maybe he fails to rescue the child from danger and some one else has to? But that would detract from him as a hero. Okay he can redeem himself, but maybe there's another way. What if the woman comes under the influence of one of her friends, who plays up the age difference angle? And if we make the age difference just on the cusp, so that it can one way or the other, so much the better.

Or what if we do it another way. What if we give *the woman* some issues. What if her ex is still hovering around in the background? Nah! Not exactly original. Or what if she's a widow, but she's still carrying a touch for dead husband. In fact maybe her husband is a bit of a hero. Maybe a cop killed in the line of duty... or a fireman... or a soldier. And maybe our engineer is plain old semi-detached suburban Mr. James.

Now that's going to make life hard for him. Even if the kid likes him. Even if the woman appreciates his "Mr Nice Guy" persona, how the hell is he going to compete with a dead war hero?

Of course there *are* ways – several ways in fact. But how we answer that question is going to shape our story. I myself found what I think was a particularly interesting way in my screenplay *Over in a Flash*.

Theme and plot

A story always has a theme. It may not always have a plot — if, for example, it is a mood piece that never really goes anywhere. But even a mood piece has a theme. It may in fact have several themes, depending on the size and scope of the plot. But it always has at least one.

For example the theme of John Grisham's *The Firm* is the struggle of a young lawyer to retain his integrity in the face of intense pressure. The theme of Tom Clancy's *The Hunt for Red October* is a man's pursuit of freedom from the clutches of a dictatorship. The theme of Agatha Christie's *Murder on the Orient Express* is the quest for justice against a man who is beyond the reach of the law. These are, to some extent, this reader's personal interpretations of the themes of those books. Other readers might find different themes in those same works, while the authors themselves might have had yet something else entirely in mind.

It is important to distinguish theme from plot. For example the plot of *The Firm*, in a nutshell, is: a young lawyer, hired at a high salary by a provincial law firm fronting for organized crime, becomes the subject of a tussle of allegiance between law enforcement officials and his corrupt employers. The plot of *The Hunt for Red October* is: a captain of a state-of-the-art Soviet submarine, seizes control of the vessel by killing the political officer and then sets off to defect to the West using the prize of his submarine as a calling card.

Note the difference between theme and plot. The theme is *what* the author is trying to say. The plot is *how* he goes about saying it. One could say that the theme is the author's "message", except that many authors would resist the suggestion that they are trying to convey a message, finding it rather too pretentious. The movie director Sam Goldwyn once dismissed a director's desire to make a musical containing a message with the words: "When I want to send a message, I'll use Western Union." But the truth of the matter is that even in the crass commercial world of Hollywood movies, messages have always abounded – and in literature even more so. A message does no have to be preachy or sermonic.

In a sense, theme comes before plot in the structural hierarchy of defining what a story *is*. The plot is an expression of the theme. This does not mean that a writer necessarily thinks of the theme before he decides on the plot. He may decide on a plot without ever thinking consciously about the theme. But the theme is almost certainly present as an undercurrent to the story.

For example if the writer conceives a plot about vigilante justice, it is quite possible that he feels that the current system of justice is inadequate or at least that society is losing confidence in the justice system because it has let them down too often. The plot then becomes the expression of this belief — the writer's vehicle for expressing his own dissatisfaction with the justice system. If this is his attitude then the story will almost certainly present the vigilante in a favorable light or at least as a desperate figure, driven to their crime by some tragic loss or by being terrorized by a villain that the law is powerless to bring to book.

Alternatively, at the other extreme, the writer may feel that public opinion is being manipulated by the press into a state of hysteria and swayed into doubting the effectiveness of judicial and police institutions that in reality are still working effectively. In that case, the story will show vigilante justice at its *worst*, portraying the vigilante as an arrogant villain or demagogue or possibly as a destructive (or self-destructive) fool.

The writer might never stop to think about his theme, preferring to focus on his plot and his characters. It is quite possible to write a first class story without ever bothering to stop and think: what's my theme? But is it good not to? Or should one, as a budding writer, think about theme as well as plot? My answer, and it is a personal one, is *yes, one **should** think about the theme*. The writer should always think about what he is trying to say and why he is trying to say it as well *how* to say it.

But that does not mean that the writer must consciously decide on his theme before embarking on the construction of a plot. Recall that I said before that theme comes before plot *in the structural hierarchy* of defining what a story *is*. This does not mean that theme comes before plot in the *chronological* hierarchy of how a story is *developed*. Writers often develop a plot and/or characters, without consciously thinking about the theme. This is especially true of writing the more commercial genres: thrillers, mystery and suspense, romance and to a lesser extent even commercial science fiction.

The question you might well ask, then, is *why* should we think about theme, as I suggested above, when we can work so well without it? The answer is because this knowledge helps us to tap and harness the creative process. Thinking about theme can restrain us from going off into flights of fancy. It can also help us to come up with that extra idea that expands short story material into the stuff of which a full-length novel is created. We can gain inspiration from our self-awareness and can also make important choices.

For example, when re-writing *A Fool for a Client* for the umpteenth time, I thought about the fact that theme of the book was the one that I gave as an example above: vigilante justice. At the plot level, the book appeared to be endorsing vigilante justice, by making the vigilante the heroine, when in fact my own feelings, as the author were rather more ambivalent. On the one hand there are some occasions when we all feel let down by the justice system. On the other hand we don't want society to degenerate into anarchy. To some extent I indicated this ambivalence by having the prosecutor make an eloquent closing argument at the trial about the dangers of vigilante justice, as well as an early discussion between him and the

District Attorney in which he confesses his doubts and sympathies with the accused, even as he struggles to cling to the conviction that he is right to prosecute her. This showed the mixed feelings that I suspect most people have about the subject.

But I felt that it wasn't enough. That was *telling* rather than *showing*. So I added a scene in which some of the villains exacted *their* version of vigilante justice on some one, to show the ugly side of the same coin. This I felt produced a balanced picture of the pros and cons of people taking the law into their own hands.

One of the best ways of learning about the relationship between theme and plot is to read several books by the same author and try to consciously identify its theme or themes.

I mentioned before a book called *The Chancellor Manuscript* by Robert Ludlum. Ludlum, also wrote another book called *The Icarus Agenda* in which a revamped version of the secretive organization, Inver Brass, appears. As in the earlier book, one of the members of Inver Brass is working towards his own agenda to the detriment of the organization and its ideals. At the end of the book, when Inver Brass is all but destroyed, one person decides to revamp it. But in recruiting his first new member, he contacts some one whom we, the readers, already know to be corrupt. Thus the cycle of secrecy followed by self-destruction is set in motion yet again. We do not need to *see* it re-enacted to know that it will be.

I also mentioned *Trevayne*, a book that Ludlum wrote under a pen-name. It described a senator who was empowered with the task of investigating defense expenditure. In the process he delves into the world of secret government. One of the characters is a sympathetically drawn Jewish arms dealer whose wife perished in the holocaust. He explains the need for the free world to be militarily strong to confront the forces of tyranny — whether left-wing or right-wing — and that if this requires secrecy and an element of corruption, that is a small price to pay to maintain the military strength of the free world.

What is the theme that binds these different books? I think it is this: that no matter how idealistic or well-meaning an organization might be, if it operates in secret, behind closed doors, it will eventually be destroyed by corruption. All it takes is a single seed of corruption and that seed will eventually grow to take over the organization and ultimately destroy its ideals. "Eternal vigilance is our only protection," the saying goes and such vigilance is only possible if the institutions that wield power are open to public scrutiny. Thus, the need for *open government* and *public accountability* is Ludlum's recurring theme.

Chapter 3 – Which genre should I write?

Genres are the way in which the publishing industry classifies books for the purposes of marketing. They are also useful for bookshops, when deciding where to display their books on the shelves. So we have thrillers, romance, science fiction, humor, literary fiction, historical fiction, true crime, celebrity biography, etc.

In the online book retail industry, they are even more useful. They can help you, the customer, search for the type of book you are looking for. They can help the online retailer (eTailer) monitor your buying habits and then offer you other books based on your tastes. This leads to a lot of sub-categorization like "legal thriller," "police procedural," etc.

But authors – and readers – do not necessarily like to be tied to particular genres. So books can also be classified using what might be called *multi*-categorization. For example a book can be a "mystery romance" or an "historical thriller" or a "science fiction comedy."

Thrillers, mystery and suspense

This is really a whole *family* of genres. That probably explains the wide variety of terms and names for the genres: mystery, suspense, crime fiction, whodunit, adventure, spy fiction, techno-thriller, police procedural, etc. Many writers specialize in just one genre within the range, some even concentrating on a regular hero who re-appears in a series of books.

In some cases these writers are professionals in other fields (law, financial trading, ex-policemen, ex-army) and are writing from experience about their own field of endeavor. However, this should deter some one who is not in that field. Thus a person who is not a lawyer, should not be afraid to write legal thrillers if they have an idea for such a story. A person who has never worn a police uniform, should not be afraid to tackle the police procedural genre. Having direct experience can be an asset, but is not a necessity. Let's take a look...

Ed McBain's 87th Precinct novels are a good example of American police procedurals, although he was never a policeman. McBain was actually a pen-name of prolific author Salvatore Albert Lombino, who legally changed his name to Evan Hunter, wrote books in a variety of genres – including the blackboard jungle – as well as being a formidable screenwriter.

John Grisham, a lawyer by training, is famous for his legal drama-thrillers. Tom Clancy, a former insurance salesman, wrote techno-thrillers featuring former Navy officer and military historian Jack Ryan. Michael Ridpath, a former trader in financial bonds, writes financial thrillers.

Going back in time, Agatha Christie wrote about a professional private detective (Hercule Poirot) and amateur private detectives (Jane Marple, Tommy and Tuppence). Former naval intelligence officer Ian Fleming wrote spy thrillers about the much-imitated but never equaled James Bond. Earle Stanley Gardner, a lawyer who got into law not via university but by working his way through the ranks as a paralegal, not only stuck to legal thrillers but wrote a series of books about one particular defense lawyer: the immortal Perry Mason.

The Perry Mason books are a particularly interesting example of how a particular discipline - in this case law – can be used as the background for a mystery novel. The Perry Mason books were essentially whodunits set against the background of a criminal trial of the wrong person. The books were very enlightening and informative as to the workings of American law, but they seldom probed the ethical complexities facing lawyers, and then none too deeply. In fact, much of what Perry Mason did, would be regarded as unethical, yet the author passed over it virtually without comment. In contrast, Grisham's legal thrillers explore complex issues of professional ethics as well as social and civic responsibility.

Some of the above writers (Gardner, Christie, Fleming, Clancy) created recurring characters. Others, like Grisham and Ridpath vary

43

their characters from book to book while sticking to the single genre that they know best. Then there are writers like Michael Crichton who explore a wide variety of genres in their novels and screenplays. Crichton has written science fiction, thrillers and created TV medical dramas in his long and distinguished career.

While the concept of "genre" should not be worn like a straight-jacket, you must be aware as a writer that online retailers – like publishers – will almost certainly try to slot your work into a genre. This does not mean that you have to force your work into a particular genre, or cut out everything hat might lead to it being categorized as belonging to another genre. But it is worth taking into account that retailers, and even readers, like to categorize. It makes them feel comfortable.

But what *are* all these thriller sub-genres? What are their distinguishing features? It might be worth taking a closer look at them, starting with the oldest.

Classic private detective (whodunit)

This genre includes both the professional private detective like Conan-Doyle's Sherlock Holmes, Agatha Christie's Hercule Poirot and Rex Stout's reclusive Nero Wolfe *and* amateur detectives like Christie's Jane Marple and Chesterton's Father Brown. The essence of the story is a murder by an unknown killer, an investigation by a detective hero or heroine and the solution announced by the detective to the assembled suspects, usually in the penultimate chapter. The final chapter is reserved for winding down the intensity of the reader's emotions and tying up the romantic loose ends.

The genre — which is as old as Edgar Alan Poe — was popularized in Britain by Arthur Conan-Doyle in the Sherlock Homes stories (most of which were published in magazines rather than as full length books. It was later developed further by Agatha Christie, Ngaio Marsh, Dorothy L Sayers and even romantic author Georgette Heyer during the nineteen twenties and thirties. Thanks mostly to Agatha Christie, it continued after the second world war into the sixties, although by then it had to compete with quite a number of other genres.

The defining feature of this genre is that the reader is invited to participate in the investigation. Although he obviously cannot ask his own questions, he is allowed to hear every question that the detective asks and see everything that the detective sees. This has great implications for the choice of the writer's point-of-view (chapter 3). What is important is that the reader is given the chance to solve the mystery *before* the detective — or at least before the detective *announces* the solution.

It is a very important requirement of the whodunit genre — almost a rule in fact — that the writer must not conceal from the reader any clues that are available to the detective. This places great demands on the writer's skill, as it is necessary to present the clues in a way that does not make them so obvious as to "spoil" the mystery.

There are various ways of doing this. One is to throw in many red-herrings along with the clues. This is perfectly legitimate as long as the red-herrings have rational alternative explanations. Another way is to present the clues through the voice or perceptions of the smart detective's proverbial side-kick. As the sidekick is less perceptive than the detective, he can notice the physical fact of the clue without his mind lighting up on it. Thus if we are being permitted to follow the sidekick's thoughts, this will not automatically give anything away. If he expresses sympathy with the colonel about his accident playing polo the week before, we might not immediate link this up with the uneven footprint pattern noted by the detective some three chapters earlier (as long as the detective didn't explicitly mention the fact that the murderer has a limp).

Yet, another way is to describe the clue in an unconventional way. In Agatha Christie's *Towards Zero*, a retired judge sought to warn a former juvenile delinquent not to return to crime by telling a group of people, including the person in question, about the person (without identifying the person or even saying that the person was present). He then said that the person had a physical peculiarity that he — the judge — would recognize anywhere. The judge died soon after in mysterious circumstances followed by the main murder and the readers were then treated to a series of red-herrings attributing physical peculiarities to practically all the characters in the story. Tucked in among these red-herrings was a scene in which the physical peculiarity was smuggled into the story so obliquely that this reader missed it completely (in spite of the fact that I am a fairly good "solutionist" of Agatha Christie whodunits). I will not give away how it was done, but if the reader's curiosity is aroused, *Towards Zero* is highly recommended.

The classic whodunit did not explore complex moral or social issues, although it was didactic within the framework of a traditionalist, conservative morality. Motives for the murder in a classic whodunit were fairly conventional violations of that traditional code of ethics: greed, envy, revenge. Usually revenge would be revenge for an illegitimate motive ("He married the woman that I loved") not retribution for a legitimate grievance ("He killed my son and then laughed at the law"). The latter would already make the story too morally complex for the genre. However, Agatha Christie did, in one of her novels, explore this theme, thereby creating a "legitimate" murder. This sort of thing would be more acceptable today, but at the time when Agatha Christie wrote the book in question, it was quite courageous.

Modern private detective stories

It is hard to write classic private detective whodunits set in the modern world, because most people now know that the police do not call in private detectives to help them investigate murders. Likewise amateur detectives who try to investigate a murder would soon find themselves hauled in by the local constabulary and have the riot act read to them (or at least the relevant law on obstructing the police). However, there are ways in which you might smuggle an amateur detective into a murder mystery as the main character and get away with it.

For example let us imagine a case in which a person is accused of a crime but his relatives insist that he is innocent and believe that there is a missing witness whom police think is a figment of their suspect's imagination. Under these circumstances, the relatives might hire a private detective to track down the missing witness. The police could hardly object to a private detective searching for a person whose very existence they dispute. Even if the police concede the possibility that the witness exists, it is not unusual for private detectives to look for missing persons.

Alternatively the private detective could be investigating employee dishonesty at a company or looking for evidence of adultery in a matrimonial dispute. If the case turns to murder, the detective would have a duty to pass on any information he possesses the police. But he could still find himself a central figure in the case. He might be playing with fire if he carries on investigating, but then again some people like to live dangerously.

There are some professional "detectives" who might be called in by the police. These are not really detectives but specialists in a scientific discipline that the police might think will be of use to them in their inquiries. For example, in those cases of murder which are not clearly "in the family", psychological profiling is becoming an increasingly common adjunct to the investigative process. Although this approach has taken a battering as a result of the Colin Stagg case, it is still common for forensic psychologists to be consulted in such cases, especially in the case of serial killers and rapists. Strictly speaking, the psychological profiler is not so much investigating the case himself as helping the police to investigate. But he could still be given a major role in the story. The TV series *Cracker* is based on this premise.

Another type of professional private "detective" who might investigate a murder case is a crime reporter. Although he too would be duty-bound to hand over to the police any information he discovers, there is no guarantee that the police will agree with the reporter as to the *significance* of the information. So it would be perfectly natural for the reporter to carry on digging until he finds enough facts to hand over the murderer's head to the police on a silver platter.

The falsely-accused suspect variation, that I mentioned above, also offers scope to the amateur detective. A close relative or friend of a falsely accused person, going out and looking for evidence to clear his relative or friend is psychologically if not functionally credible. By that I mean that even if there are very few people who would have the time to drop everything and start investigating to save some one close to them from the jaws of injustice, most people would *want* to do so if one of their loved ones or trusted friends was falsely (in their opinion) accused. In that sense it does not strain the readers credulity in *psychological* terms. If the writer can construct circumstances which would give the protagonist *time* to investigate, this premise could be turned into a credible story.

Tough Streetwise detective

This genre – also known as the "hard-boiled" private investigator – is the American variation on the private detective theme. Whereas the "private *detective*" in a British story is characterized most strongly by his mind, the American private "investigator" (or PI) is characterized by that quintessentially American virtue "toughness". He may be small (like the actor Humphrey Bogart), but he is *tough*. He is good in a fight, and even if he gets the crap kicked out of him, he doesn't back down. He just wakes up with a lump on his forehead, with his pretty receptionist holding an ice-pack to it!

His British (or Belgian) counterpart would probably be smart enough not to get himself into that situation in the first place – or if he did, he would talk his way out of it. Actually, that is a trifle unfair. The British detective operates in a different environment. The classic private detective story in Britain is set in a quiet country house (with secret passages) or a pleasant little rural village with wicker fences and garden parties, where tea is served in bone china cups by quaint old ladies. In such environments, violence is almost unknown, apart from the murder itself, which is almost invariably a carefully premeditated act and not a spontaneous eruption of violence. Also, in such stories, the actual murder is hardly ever narrated. Instead, we hear "shouts" and then a body is "discovered". Even *that* assumes that the victim was bludgeoned to death rather than shot... or poisoned.

48

The hard-boiled American PI, in contrast operates in the tough, gritty world of the mean streets of the inner city, which are governed by a different set of rules to the rustic villages of middle England. If our gentlemanly English detective in his cloak and deer stalker ever found himself in an American inner city ghetto, he would probably waste no time at all in getting himself trapped in some back ally by a street urchin who looks younger than the Artful Dodger but acts more like Bill Sykes! And if our hero relies on the "noble art" of fisticuffs to get himself out of a tight spot, he's quite likely to find that the ten-year-old who's after his wallet is "packing a rod."

Such an unlikely juxtaposition of cultures could make for a very good comic thriller, like the TV movie about a man in New York who gets hit on the head and develops the delusion that he is Sherlock Holmes!

This brings us to another point: the protagonist of an American hard-boiled detective may not have the English detective's finely-honed, sophisticated intellect, but he does possess a wisdom of his own: street wisdom. The term "streetwise" could almost have been coined to describe the American hard-boiled detective.

The hard-boiled detective may well be called in for something other than to investigate a murder. He might be asked to bring back some rich man's daughter from the no-goodnik that she's run off with. He might be asked to retrieve some valuable artifact. But whatever the starting point for the story, it usually results in murder.

The hard-boiled investigator genre was pioneered by Dashiel Hammet and Raymond Chandler, and later developed by James Hadley Chase and Mickey Spillane. As with the British detective genre, one finds both writers who create one or more recurring characters (Mickey Spillane with Tiger Mann and Mike Hammer) and writers like James Hadley Chase who created different characters with each story, including some particularly odious ones (like the vindictive Ma Grissom in *No Orchids for Miss Blandish*).

The genre is very much movie-oriented in the sense that it is heavy on narration and light on description. There is plenty of dialogue , but in short bursts. Dialogue in a hard-boiled American detective story must be crackling like fireworks not flowing like a river.

Another salient feature of the genre is that it lacks any sense of optimism. The mystery is solved, but the ending is frequently not happy. Of course strictly speaking the ending can never be happy where murder is concerned. Even if the murderer is brought to justice, the victim is still dead. And if the victim is himself or herself a wrongdoer, then the damage that *they* did remains done, notwithstanding *their* death. Thus it is inescapable to get away from at least some unhappiness in a murder story.

But the hard-boiled American detective story is all too frequently characterized by giving the reader even less moral satisfaction than its British counterpart. In the hard-boiled detective genre it is quite possible for the murderer to be identified but not brought to justice. This might be because he is too rich and powerful or because the evidence is insufficient to convict, or because of legal technicalities in the way the evidence was obtained that guarantee that he cannot be convicted. The reader's curiosity is satisfied but his sense of justice is not. In some cases, the villain is able to set-up some one else to take the rap. The hero may know this but be powerless to prove it in court — or not dare to challenge so powerful a figure as the villain when he is finally identified. Thus the reader's sense of moral propriety is frustrated by the denouement, instead of fulfilled.

Before we leave our tough, streetwise American PI, one other important distinction between him and his genteel British counterpart needs to be mentioned: the American PI is not burdened by the ethical code of the gentleman (or lady) detective this side of the pond. For example, whereas the British detective must rely on guile to extract information from an uncooperative witness, our transatlantic hero is perfectly free to threaten to "bust the ass" of the reluctant witness and even to follow through on the threat.

This is only one example. The hard-boiled hero is exempt from most of the rules of ethics. He can cheat on his wife, sleep with a client's wife, go on a drinking binge and wake up in the gutter, cheat at cards and use violence against people who are not themselves the villains of the piece. He should not murder the innocent — although if he executes a murderer or rapist in cold blood, he is still within the rules of the genre. He could frequent prostitutes and be into S and M, or even be gay (albeit of a "macho" sort). On the other hand there are limits. For example, he cannot be a pedophile without turning into a villain rather than merely a flawed hero. He can be a bastard, but not a *sick* bastard.

Police detective – British

This genre brings us one step closer to realism. In real life it is of course the police who investigate murders and other serious crimes, not tough American Private Investigators and not country vicars or elderly antiques experts.

The police detective story can show how the police really investigate a crime. The hero could be either the police officer who heads the investigation, or some young dynamic junior officer who steals the show. They might the young protégé of the senior officer being groomed for greater things to follow or they may be the thorn in the side of the crusty old superior who has become something of a stereotype.

Examples of the police detective genre include Ruth Rendell's Inspector Wexford, P. D. James's Adam Dalgleish and Colin Dexter's Inspector Morse. Earlier examples include John Creasey's Inspector West and Gideon of the Yard (whom the prolific Creasey created under the pseudonym J.J. Maric).

The genre provides excellent opportunities to writers who like to do their research thoroughly. There is a lot to learn about SOCOs (Scene of Crimes Officers) who gather the physical evidence and the command chain of the police if one wants to write a realistic police detective mystery.

DNA for example is not as straightforward a matter as many people think. There are now techniques for increasing the quantity of a minute sample of DNA by heating it in the presence of enzymes. The existing DNA forms a template on which mirror strands form.

51

There is also a method for getting useful DNA from hair samples *without* a follicle (root). In the past they needed the root because it contained a nucleus with the full DNA of the person from whom the hair comes. But even hair without a root contains something called "mitochondrial DNA". This is the DNA that comes only from the mother of the person rather than the full set which contains the DNA that the person got from both parents. With mitochondrial DNA they can identify a hair as belonging to a particular set of siblings who have the same mother. But they cannot say which sibling the hair belongs to.

It is important to keep up with such developments if one wants to be sure of writing a credible (and topical) police detective mystery. It is also important to know how the police go about lifting fingerprints from a crime scene, how they compare fingerprints, how many points of comparison are needed to declare that fingerprints match, how they use mugshots (it's different in Britain from the way they do it in America) and much, much more.

Police procedural – mainly American

Closely related to the police detective is the police procedural. This type of story is also about the workings of the police, but whereas a police detective novel focuses on one particular investigation, a police procedural is often a saga with multiple story lines. There might be to or three investigations described in the book and others alluded to more obliquely.

In a police procedural there might indeed be a serious crime in one of the story lines. But it is never permitted to dominate the story. It is shown to co-exist with the more mundane aspects of police work. The serious crime might never be resolved in this type of fiction (giving it a note of gritty realism), or as in the tough PI genre it might be resolved for the purpose of reader's knowledge but without the miscreant being brought to justice. Then again, the reader might be told in advance who committed the crime in a multi-viewpoint story and then shown how the police try to solve it, along with their other work.

The real subject of a police procedural is how the police work rather than the solution to a particular crime. The main characters are not the perpetrator's or victims of the crime but rather the police themselves as they go about their business, interact with the public, the press and the system. It is a quintessentially American genre, the most prominent practitioner of which is Ed McBain. It has also invaded our TV screens in the form of series like *Hill Street Blues*, *NYPD* and in a more home grown variety, *The Bill*.

Much of the technical detail that is relevant to the police detective mystery also applies to the police procedural. Research is perhaps even more important in the police procedural as one has to get *everything* right, and there is far more factual ground covered in a police procedural with parallel story lines than a police detective story with just one. In a police procedural, even such mundane matters as when they change shifts become important. Of course, the writer might be tempted to say, "well the average reader won't know that." And perhaps the average editor won't either — although I wouldn't count on it. But even if you can get it past the editor and even if almost all the readers miss it, the fact is that sloppy research is sloppy research. And if you're planning to make it *your* genre, it pays to get it right. Otherwise sooner or later your reputation will become tarnished.

Historical thriller

The historical thriller is a real intellectual challenge to the writer and can provide great intellectual stimulation to the reader. It is very much a "thinking person's" genre, although that is not to belittle the other genres.

Historical thrillers can include both the investigation of a past mystery and mysteries set in the past.

One of the most famous historical thrillers is Dan Brown's *Da Vinci Code*, preceded by *Angels and Demons*, and followed by *The Lost Symbol* and *Inferno*. My own books *The Moses Legacy* and *The Boudicca Parchments* (written under the pen-name Adam Palmer) are in the same tradition: modern conspiracy thrillers with an historical connection.

A more straightforward example of an historical thriller (if one can really call it straightforward) is Umberto Eco's *The Name of the Rose*. This is not just a murder mystery set at a monastery but also a novel offering insight into the history of the Catholic Church. In similar vein, a whole series of historical thrillers has been written by Ellis Peters. Her detective hero is a twelfth century monk called Brother Cadfael.

My sister — who has a master's degree in classical studies — was once planning to write a series of murder mysteries set in ancient Rome. The hero of the story was to be the Urban Prefect, the closest thing they had to a policeman.

The other form of historical thriller genre involves retrospective analysis of an ancient crime. The most famous example of this was Josephine Tey's *The Daughter of Time*, in which a police officer, while recuperating in hospital, "investigates" the murder of the "princes in the tower," a crime allegedly attributed to Richard III. This was not just a made up background, but rather a genuine historical mystery and is the subject of an ongoing dispute among historians.

The historical context to the story is a dispute over the throne of England between Henry Tudor (Henry VII) and Richard III. The princes imprisoned in the Tower of London were in line for the throne and their death cleared the way for either Henry or Richard (although even after the death's of Richard and the princes, there were said to be 22 people in line for the throne ahead of Henry VII). Anyway to cut a long story short, Henry defeated Richard in battle, had himself declared king from the day before the battle (so that anyone who had opposed him could be said to have been guilty of treason) and history recorded that it was the evil hunchback Richard III who had the princes killed. With Richard in the frame, Henry was in the clear.

This view was most eloquently expressed by Shakespeare. However many people have questioned that view and suggested that this is a case of history being written by the winners. Shakespeare, although a writer of great skill, was nevertheless dependent on Royal patronage and it has been suggested that he colluded in the rewriting of history to endear himself to his Tudor patrons.

In Josephine Tey's novel, the police detective "investigates" the crime and concludes, on the basis of some compelling evidence that the Tudor version is false and that Henry VII and not Richard III was responsible for having the princes killed. This does not involve the discovery of new evidence as much as reinterpreting the existing evidence. It is, in effect, an historical thesis narrated in a work of fiction.

The reason I have given such a lengthy description of this book is to show how one can create a fascinating piece of work by combining fact and fiction. It is not perhaps the most lucrative of genres, unless ones book is truly superb and manages to capture the attention of the reviewers in a big way. But for those who are interested in history and want to bring it to life, and who are ready to do thorough research, it offers great scope and potential.

One of the Inspector Morse mysteries also had it's hero investigating a murder from the past, although it was a made up mystery rather than a real historical event. This too is an interesting spin on the historical thriller genre and also requires thorough research as one must still understand the culture and mores of the time, as well as getting the dialogue right and free of anachronisms.

Suspense

Suspense is in many ways the opposite of mystery. Whereas in mystery, one of the characters knows something that the readers don't know, in suspense the reader's frequently know something that the her or heroine does *not*. This is a more serious version of the "look behind you" phenomenon that we see in comic form in a Christmas pantomime. Strictly speaking not all suspense involved the hero/heroine being ignorant of the danger. Sometimes they are well aware of he danger, but the question is whether or not they will be able to deal with it.

This of course leads to one of the sub-genres of suspense fiction: the "Woman in Jeopardy" story. In a woman in jeopardy story, the underlying premise is usually the greater supposed vulnerability of women in comparison with men. Even in the feminist era this sort of fiction thrived and it continues to enjoy popularity in the post-feminist era. Part of the reason for the enduring popularity of this genre is the equal but different capacity of male and female readers to relate to the heroine. Male readers may feel attracted towards her or even protective, wishing that they could jump into the story and protect her. Female readers may identify with her, especially as in most of the novels of this genre, the heroine is an ordinary women in an ordinary job, who finds herself confronted with an extraordinary situation.

Most people look for excitement in their lives, and the capacity to enjoy someone else's excitement vicariously, but without the attendant dangers, is something that many readers will appreciate. Not that the heroine will share there emotions. The "jeopardy" — so exciting to the readers in *their* mundane jobs — is no source of joy to the heroine, because she hasn't got the time to stop and enjoy the adventure. She's too busy trying to stay alive.

Another type of suspense thriller that may in some cases overlap with Woman in Jeopardy is the "chase thriller". In this sub-genre, the hero or heroine is chased by some enemy seeking to destroy or capture them. This may be because they have seen something or know something that they shouldn't.

It might also be that they have something that some one else wants, a document or a scientific contraption. This variation of the chase sub-genre is sometimes called "chase the widget". It was popularized by American TV afternoon serials in the 1960s. Although not as common now as it used to be, the genre is still around today and there are some very good examples of it. In effect, Tom Clancy's *The Hunt for Red October* was a chase the widget thriller, albeit on a grand scale. It was the fascinating characterizations and character motivations that made it several cuts above the average.

Another type of chase-suspense thriller is the "killer on the loose" variety. In this genre a killer is out there and has to be stopped. He may already have seized his next intended victim (as in William McGivern's *Night of the Juggler* and Thomas Harris's *The Silence of the Lambs*) or he may simply be highly-motivated assassin working his way down a list (as in Joseph DiMona's *Last Man at Arlington* or my own *Reckless Justice*).

Legal thriller/courtroom drama

One hardly needs to define the legal thriller genre as we all know what it is. It has evolved somewhat over the years, since the early days of Perry Mason in the 1930s. as I mentioned at the start of this chapter, the Perry Mason mysteries were mystery stories set against a background of a criminal trial. But they did offer a glimpse into the cut and thrust of adversarial courtroom proceedings and paved the way for others to follow.

Over the years a number of writers have contributed to this genre including Clifford Irving, Scott Turow, John Grisham and Brad Melzer. All of these are in America. In Britain the genre is not so highly developed, although British legal thrillers are starting to appear. My own *A Fool for a Client* was a modest contribution to that genre. Although I am British, the book was set in the United States and was generously described by one reviewer as "a workmanlike piece of entertainment for Grisham fans with withdrawal symptoms."

Since then two of my books with British settings have also had one foot in the legal thriller camp. Both *The Other Victim* and *Reckless Justice* had significant portions set in court. In *The Other Victim* it was a committal hearing in a magistrates court. In *Reckless Justice* it was a criminal trial for rape and murder at the Old Bailey. The reason I mention this is because notwithstanding my earlier warning about writing cross-genre fiction, it is possible to span more than one genre and get away with it. Both those two books were police detective thrillers and techno-thrillers in addition to being legal thrillers.

The foremost exponent of the legal-thriller/courtroom-drama genre in Britain at the moment is Rankin Davis, who is actually two writers.

Political thriller

This genre offers the best possibility to do double duty as quality literature as well as being "a good read." The political thriller can deal with the machinations of politicians themselves or about Machiavellian intrigue among civil servants. It can be about attempts by press barons to subvert the political process by hijacking public opinion or it can be about the interaction between these disparate forces.

One excellent example of a political thriller that combines all of these elements is Edward Stewart's *They've Shot the President's Daughter* about an elaborate plot involving blackmail and spin doctoring to abolish the Bill of Rights in the USA (i.e. the first ten amendments to the constitution) and to persuade public opinion to accept it, by playing on fear of crime. Irving Wallace's *The R Document*, explores a similar theme. In Britain, Michael Dobbs's *House of Cards*, gave the political thriller genre a satiric twist.

Political thrillers however run the risk of not being easily transportable across the Pond. The reason for this is that in Britain we have a professional civil service in which the most senior members have lifetime tenure. In the United States, by contrast, the top layers of civil servants are "political appointees" who change from one presidential administration to the next. Thus, an American reader might find it hard to understand senior civil servants plotting against their political masters, while a British reader might not be able to follow why the relations between the politicians and the civil servants are so harmonious.

Of course problems of transatlantic understanding are not insurmountable. The writer can explain the way the system works in the narrative and make the book all the more interesting in the process. The well-researched "information novel" can be a pleasure to read as long as the reader is not overloaded with "information" at the expense of the story.

Spy thriller

This can be a variant of the political thriller, but doesn't have to be. It can be anything from the escapism of Ian Fleming's James Bond to the realism of Len Deighton and John le Carre. The background must of course move with the times. In the thirties it may well have been the gray clouds of Nazism and fascism looming on the horizon. In the forties, the Second World War itself would have provided the backdrop. In the fifties and sixties, the cold war would have provided the stage on which the drama would have unfolded. Then in the seventies it would have been the emergent powers of oil states and regional disputes that threatened to escalate into global conflicts. In the eighties, it might have returned to eastern Europe as the wind of change swept in with the change of generation among the leadership.

It is up to the writer to decide how to modernize the genre to suit the current era. Aside from numerous regional conflicts and the toppling of long-standing dictatorships, we now see the rise of militant and extreme Islam. At the other end of the spectrum, we get the paranoid conspiracy theories about Zionism, the Illuminati, the Freemasons, the CIA and the " New World Order." Many of these are deeply offensive to rational people – some even bordering on hate-mongering – but for good or for ill, they have become a staple of the thriller market.

Techno-thriller

The techno-thriller is a specialized form of the information novel. It can be a variant of the political thriller or of the spy thriller. It can also be a suspense thriller of the "chase the widget" variety. It can also be a financial thriller in which hi-tech meets high-finance.

The essence of the techno-thriller is of course technology. This can be anything from computers and electronic devices to lasers, to bombs, to computer software.

The thrillers of Tom Clancy are, for the most part, techno-thrillers. *The Hunt for Red October* was about a Lithuanian defector who sets out to flee from the Soviet Union in a state-of-the-art submarine that is propelled by a method called "magnetohydrodynamics". That long-winded term simply means that it propels itself by passing electric currents through a hollow channel running along the length of the hull.

One of the most topical backgrounds for techno-thrillers today is the fast-changing world of computers in general and the Internet in particular. Viruses, hacking into sensitive systems, using hi-tech computers and software in crime solving (e.g. to detect a pattern of a serial killer or to graphically reconstruct the aged face of a killer from the past) – all these offer great scope for thriller writers today.

As with any other information novel, the difference between the best and the worst is that the best give just enough technical information to make the story understandable, the worst indulges in excess by showing off how much research the writer has done, slowing down the story in the process.

Strictly speaking, the techno-thriller almost invariably belongs to at least one other genre. In stories of conflict between nations it is a spy thriller or a political one. If it is a chase the widget story it is suspense. If it is about the use of technology to stop crime it may be a detective story or a police procedural. If it is about a dispute over the quality of scientific evidence it may be a legal thriller. But sometimes the emphasis is so heavily on the technology that it becomes a techno-thriller first and the other genre second. If the writer is comfortable with technology and enjoys explaining it to the lay reader it is a fine genre to write and an enjoyable one to read.

Non-thriller genres

As I am principally a thriller writer, this book focuses mainly on the various genres of thriller. However, as most of the book is about writing fiction in general – or at least in broader terms – it is worth doing a quick review of other genres.

Science Fiction and fantasy

Like thrillers, this is a whole family of genres, including dystopian, apocalyptic, space-opera, time-travel, parallel universe, alternative history, space-military, technology-run-amok, steam-punk, cyberpunk and a whole host of others. Even in the "categories" above, there is a fair amount of overlap.

In recent years a new market has opened up: the teenage female market. I am not saying that there were no books for teenagers before. But in the internet and Kindle age, this market has exploded into something huge. From the proliferation of vampire books to the *Hunger Games*, this market has become **HUGE!** Part of the reason is that teenage girls have always read more than their male counterparts. Add to this the lowering of the cost per book. Just as the paperback heralded a new age of cheap books, the Amazon Kindle and the proliferation of tablets and large screen smart phones, has brought down the cost further, aided authors in building up their markets directly (thereby removing the traditional gatekeepers- and arbiters of quality) and in conjunction with the internet created a rapid-fire word-of-mouth marketing that operates faster than any village gossip!

Particularly popular in this teenage (female) market are vampire stories in which the girl falls for the young male vampire and tries to save or tame him. In these stories, the male vampire is the stand-in for the bad boy who needs to be tamed. This is an old theme: man as the animal, woman as the agent of his salvation.

This leads to...

Romance

This genre includes classic romance of Jane Austen, the faux-historical novels of twentieth century writers, the innocent but modern romances published by Harlequin or Mills & Boone and the modern-day chick-lit which comments on the modern woman's role in society, the way she sees herself and the way others treat her. The

Bridget Jones series and the *Shopaholic* books by Sophie Kinsella are the leading examples of this genre.

Historical fiction

Aside from historical thrillers, there is a whole genre of historical fiction, usually focusing on fictitious characters in real historical events.

Literary fiction

One has only to look at the Booker Prize shortlist to see that literary fiction is alive and well. From Salman Rushdie to Donna Tarte, from Kate Mosse to Hilary Mantel, the genre is alive and well.

Erotica, soft-core pornography, etc.

In the modern world, these genres have become respectable. To some extent, they have been since the nineteen fifties, with books like *Peyton Place* and the novels of Harold Robins, Jacqueline Susann and Jackie Collins. But the taking of the restraints has – paradoxically – unleashed a wave of books like *Fifty Shades of Grey* and a whole host of imitations.

Choosing the right genre

All right, so you've got the basic plot of story… and you understand the concept of genre. Now you face a tough decision. You have to decide how you're going to write your story. Is it going to be a detective story, a psychological novel or a suspense story.

Choosing in relation to plot

Sometimes the genre of the story is dictated naturally by the plot of the story as it is conceived by the writer. If the writer thinks of a man being murdered by drowning in the lake of a quiet village while a garden party is in progress at the mansion of the local big-wig, that suggests an amateur private detective, possibly in the style of Agatha

Christie. If the first thing that comes to mind is a young woman who works for a large multinational company being hounded by a cyber-stalker in the same company, that is obviously a suspense story of the *woman-in-jeopardy* sub-genre. But there are plots that can be written in different ways and as such in different genres.

Cutting across genres

Consider the case of a man accused of rape and murder on a basis of DNA evidence that is stored in a database which may have been tampered with by a hacker. The emphasis could be placed on the police investigation, with one police officer having his doubts about the evidence. That would make it a police detective or police procedural story. It could follow the accusation through to the criminal trial, as the defense lawyer tries to argue away the evidence — making it into a courtroom drama. Alternatively, the story might focus on the hacker and his nefarious activities, playing mind-games with the reader as to his motives. This would make it a techno-thriller or a psychological one.

But that's only the beginning. As we talked about before, the falsely accused man might have a close relative who believes in his innocence and is frantically looking for the evidence, thus turning the story into a modernised version of the amateur private detective. Or the lawyer might hire another hacker to investigate the possibility of tampering with the computer system— thus putting the story into a modern variant of the professional private investigator genre. Or then again an intrepid reporter might take up the cudgels on behalf of the accused, like Emile Zola taking up the cause of Dreyfus and Arthur Conan-Doyle campaigning for the release of Oscar Slater.

We can take this idea even further afield. If the accused man is a politician and he is being fitted up to discredit him, then we have a political thriller. Or perhaps he is a government scientist and is being framed to clear the way for an agent of a foreign power to get his job. They could just assassinate him, but that would set off alarm bells and would inevitably provoke a security investigation. On the other hand, if he goes down because of apparent personal character flaws then they wouldn't be so worried about his successor's security clearance, only that he is in a stable one-to-one relationship with an equally level-headed woman. Then it becomes a spy thriller.

Selecting the genre you're comfortable with

Thus, we see, there are stories that might easily fit into more than one genre, possibly two or more at the same time. The author does not necessarily need to select a genre. He can simply write the story as it occurs to him and let others categorize it. But even if he does not select a *genre*, he must still decide *how* to tell the story.

In the story above, for example, does he focus on the falsely accused man and the investigators (amateur and professional) while keeping the hacker in the background? Does he reveal the hacker's identity early on or does he leave the reader to speculate as to whether or not the hacker is real and thus whether or not the accused man is guilty? Does he make the hacker the rapist, or is the hacker merely an opportunist with his own agenda? (If so then there are *two* mysteries in the book: who is the rapist and why is the hacker fitting up an innocent man?) Does the writer let the case come to trial or does he set the entire story in the police investigative phase of the proceedings? Or does he have the accused charged and then have the events unfold while the accused is on remand awaiting trial? Do the police solve the riddle or does some one else have to force them to recognize that they have been misled?

There is no hard and fast answer to the questions above. They are questions that obviously need an answer before you proceed to write. But there is no *right* answer, or at least no answer that is *objectively* right. There are however many wrong answers. The wrong answers are any of the styles that you don't feel comfortable with. This in turn implies that the *right* answer is that one that you *do* feel most comfortable with. This does not mean that writing is a comfortable act. But you should write in a genre that you find interesting and that falls within the scope of your ability. This does not mean you have to be a lawyer to write legal thrillers or a police officer to write police procedurals. It just means that writing the story should be the intellectual equivalent or a vigorous full-body workout; *not* a tiring but mundane chore. It should be like pumping iron rather than cleaning the windows.

Effect of the choice of genre

Of course once you select the genre you will be embarking on a certain road from which you cannot easily divert to another except by retracing your footsteps and starting again. The choice of genre affects a whole host of other variables.

How the genre influences the development of the basic idea

As we have noted, different genres go with different forms of story-telling. The choice of genre impacts upon how much emphasis we place on the characters, whose viewpoint we use when telling the story and even how we resolve the story.

If we decide on a legal thriller we have to take the case to trial. By that stage the police will not be doing any further investigating unless compelled to do so. For example, if a person comes forward purporting to have new evidence, the police must check out the alleged new evidence. But they will not re-open the investigation while the trial is in progress just because one of the police officers is not satisfied with the quality of the evidence. But some one outside the police might.

If you have decided on a suspense thriller in which the question is whether or not the malicious hacker or the falsely accused man and his friends will *prevail against the adverse circumstances*, then you cannot *also* make it a mystery in which the man's *innocence or guilt is at issue*. Well... actually you can, but it would be quite complicated.

Supposing on the other hand, some one is investigating on behalf of the accused. Then we will have to follow them, at least part of the time and see how they progress in their investigation. On the other hand if it is to be a police detective story, then it must be set before the trial and we must give the police a reason for *not* being satisfied with the quality of DNA evidence that is normally considered so reliable (e. g. the DNA says he's guilty but he appears to have a rock-solid alibi offered by apparently disinterested parties).

How the choice of genre influences the character types

Just as the way in which the plot unfolds is affected by the choice of genre, so are the character types. For example if the basis of the story is to be that an intrepid reporter takes up the case, then our central character is going to be a reporter who is determined and single-minded. The police for their part will be conservative and skeptical — although it would be a mistake to make them stupid as that would turn them into dated stereotypes.

If the story focuses on the police investigation and their efforts to resolve the contradictions in the evidence, then the story could explore the character conflicts among the police team, including differences of attitude between men and women, and perhaps conflicts across the lines of authority, showing the scope of dissent within the police.

Every genre has certain character types that belong to it naturally. The amateur detective must always be an expert in something other than detection. It can be ornithology or music, or antiques. He could be a dentist or an architect. But he must possess a specialization that gives color and dimension to his character. The hard-boiled detective must be just that: hard-boiled. The legal thriller must have some one connected with the law. It need not be a lawyer. It could be a judge who is supposed to sit there on high while others present the evidence, deciding – against all the rules of his profession – that he's going to investigate the case himself. Or it could be a paralegal or solicitor's representative, who thinks that everyone else has missed something but who is not taken seriously when he or she tries to draw their attention to it.

We will discuss this further in the chapter on Characterization.

The impact of the different genres on the readers psyché

Finally, the choice of genre affects the reader's mind.

A police investigation will have the reader guessing, but leave them confident that the system works. If the accused is charged or the case goes all the way to trial, it will leave the reader worried about the prospects for justice in the real world. An investigative story will have the reader's scratching their heads mystified over what is going on. On the other hand if the story is demystified by making it clear that the evidence was tampered with and turning it into a suspense story with the hero and villain dueling over the outcome, then the readers will be sitting on the edge of their seats wondering not "what's happening?" but rather "What's *going* to happen?"

Although writer's are free to choose the genre without considering what impact it will have on the reader, they might wish to factor the psychological impact of the choice of genre into the equation. If the writer *wants* to challenge the reader's intellect they might make the novel a puzzle mystery. If they want the readers sitting on the edge of their seats, biting their nails, writers will go for suspense.

A writer may also be thinking of the movie rights, knowing that a puzzle mystery makes for good television, but an action thriller makes for good widescreen cinema. This is a perfectly legitimate consideration for the writer to take into account.

Ultimately, the choice is yours and should be based on what interests you to write and what you enjoy. But when you are making the decision, be aware of its consequences on the project as a whole.

Chapter 4 – How should I go about *telling* the story?

Anatomy of a novel

A novel (be it thriller, mystery, suspense, romance, science fiction, historical, literary, fantasy or any other genre) has a number of aspects. What is the theme? What is the story? How is it told? These different facets are all present, super-imposed one upon the other. To understand the inner workings of a thriller it is worth taking a closer look at them.

Theme and dramatic situation

We have already talked about theme, but let us explore further.

Inspired by a remark of another writer, Georges Polti in a seminal work of 1868 (*The Thirty Six Dramatic Situations*) sought to classify all the dramatic themes that could occur in a literary or dramatic work. I will not try to recreate that work here, beyond saying that the book, which draws heavily on ancient Greek and Shakespearean drama, comes highly recommended. Some of its categories are extremely useful in discussing and analyzing thrillers and their elements.

Strictly speaking, what Polti classified were not themes of the entire story but the essentials of dramatic situations, as the title implies. As with theme, a story may contain more than one dramatic situation. While theme and dramatic situation are not identical, I will use the terms interchangeably for this stage of the analysis.

With this in mind, let us consider Agatha Christie's *Towards Zero*. It was about three things:

- a killer who was motivated by *revenge*

- the investigative efforts to *catch that killer*, and

- the *rescue of an innocent suspect* from the prospect of wrongful conviction for murder.

How does this translate into Polti's schema of dramatic situations?

If we focus on the *rescue* of the innocent suspect, the theme of the story is "Deliverance" — No. 2 in Polti's classification system. The essential elements of the Deliverance theme are: an *Unfortunate*, a *Threatener* and a *Rescuer*. The Threatener can of course be a force of nature rather than a person, but in a thriller it is most likely to be a person.

But before Agatha Christie took the story into the final stage of Deliverance, she made it clear that the falsely accused had already reached the stage of "Falling Prey to Cruelty or Misfortune" — No. 7 in Polti's schema. At one point in the story, the innocent suspect pleads for help, thus bringing in "Supplication" (No. 1 in Polti's schema), the elements of which are a *Supplicant* and a *Power* in authority. The false accusation also falls within the category of Erroneous Judgement (No. 33)

Thus the story of the innocent suspect alone contains at least *four* of Polti's dramatic situations!

Turning to the villain of the piece, and the motives behind the villain's actions, we find a veritable Chinese restaurant menu of dramatic situations. There is Adultery (No. 25), Rivalry (No. 24) Murderous Adultery (No. 15), Rivalry of Kinsman (No. 14), Vengeance upon Kindred (No. 4), Madness (No. 16).

Finally if we focus on the efforts of the police detective to solve the mystery and identify the murderer, the theme becomes "Crime Pursued by Vengeance" (No. 3). But it is also related to "Enigma" (No. 11), the elements of which are an *Interrogator*, a *Seeker* and *Problem*. The theme of Crime Pursued by Vengeance also applies to the villain's motives in the story. This does not mean that the villain has been the victim of crime or wrongdoing *objectively*, but rather *subjectively*: a wrong has been done to the villain *from the villain's point of* view and must be avenged.

This example illustrates how even a relatively short book, with a singular, integrated plot, can have several dramatic themes. But in many novels there is usually one dominant theme, which might be called the main emphasis of the story as a whole. Below is a listing, by no means exhaustive, of themes that are to be found in many novels:

1. An effort to bring a wrongdoer to justice.
2. An attempt at self-vindication or vindication of a third party.
3. The quest for self-fulfilment (including, of course, the quest for fortune).
4. The quest for freedom.
5. The quest for justice in general.
6. An attempt to negate or neutralise a source of natural or man-made danger.
7. An efforts to understand something even if one cannot do anything about it.
8. Muddling along without hope because it is one's job.
9. The quest for a relationship with a desired individual.
10. The quest to help another.

These should be taken as generic themes to be fleshed out by the writer. For example, the theme of a police thriller might be to catch a criminal or rescue a victim. The theme of a science fiction novel might be to overthrow tyranny. The theme of a rite-of-passage novel might be to win a sporting event... or to learn something about life from *not* winning. The theme of a romance might be a woman seeking to marry the man of her dreams. (Ugh!)

Structure

It is important for a novel to have a structure. But as to *what* sort of structure, that is very much up to you – the author – to decide. "Very much"? Well, let me rephrase that: the author has a certain amount of discretion. The Russian-American author Ayn Rand, argued that them motto of the architect Louis Sullivan was very much applicable to books: "Form follows function."

A book should have a beginning, a middle and an end. But that does not mean that the facts have to be related in chronological order. That is, the beginning of the *story* does not have to be the beginning of the *book*. You can jump in to the middle of the story or even begin the story at the end. Sidney Sheldon began two of his most successful books (*The Other Side of Midnight* and *Stranger in the Mirror*) with prologues that were set either at or close to the end of the story, and then took the reader back to the events leading up to them. Indeed a whole story can be told completely out of order, like the Tarantino movie *Pulp Fiction*.

Robert Ludlum's *The Icarus Agenda* jumps into the middle of a story after a group of people have been taken hostage by a bunch of political extremists. Richard Condon's *Death of a Politician* starts with the murder of a Richard Nixon like politician in 1964 (instead of him becoming president four years later) and then alternates between the official police investigation and flashback reminiscences about the politician by his various acquaintances under drug-induced hypnosis in a parallel investigation by a secretive government agency. Thus the writer has great latitude in how to structure and pace his stories.

Tarantino notwithstanding, the practice of playing around with the order of events in a story is more easily managed in a book than in movies. The reason for this is that in a book, the reader can always re-read if the author's technique leads to any confusion. While this may not be ideal, at least the option is there.

In contrast, in the movies, people have to rely on memory and if the story is told out of order, it leads to confusion for which the audience has no remedy. I remember one occasion when I was watching an old film called *Johnny Got his Gun*, an anti-war story scripted by Dalton Trumbo based on his novel of the same title. The projectionist (this was at a special showing) somehow managed to get the reels in the wrong order and showed one of the later scenes earlier. It was only much later — when he showed the reel that continued from that reel — that the audience realized that something had gone wrong.

However even after the movie, when we were leaving the cinema, heard people talking about the incident as if the projectionist had shown an *earlier* reel *too late* rather than the other way round. In other words, they wrongly assumed that the reel that took up where the first reel left off should have been shown earlier. It was only because I had read the book that I knew that they were wrong. It was rather the *earlier* reel that should have been shown *later.*

For this reason it should be clear why playing around with the order of events and generally going against the chronology of events is rare in the movies, except when it is a clear-cut flashback designed to reveal the solution to a mystery. One screenwriter, cited the example of the movie *High* Noon to show how it is possible to make a movie that has a back story without even showing *one* flashback. However, the only way in which this can be accomplished is by *telling* rather than showing – when the golden rule is movies and books alike is actually: *show, don't tell!*

So the writer of a novel should feel free to play around with the order of presentation if that is what the story calls for. One can do play with the order in which events are presented in order to mystify, surprise, confuse or excite the reader.

But this also another reason one might want to do so. And that is to present the back-story. If thee back story is long and involved – and there is a danger that presenting it in one block at the start of the story, might give the novel a "slow" feel, then you can work the background into the novel gradually in fragments, distributed throughout the narrative. The important thing to remember is that at any given stage the readers should have enough information to understand the things that they are *meant* to understand. (It goes without saying that there may be some events that they are *not* yet meant to understand.)

Questions put to the reader

From the above it can be seen that there are a small number of recurrent themes in mystery and suspense writing. But in addition to the small choice of themes there is a large choice of methods of presentation. The writer can approach the issue of *how* to tell his story in a variety of ways.

First of all, it is worth remembering that when the readers are reading, there are questions going through their minds. Typical questions that might arise are:

1. Who did what?
2. Why did they do it?
3. What were/are/will-be the consequences of what they did?

These are questions that the writer is effectively putting into the reader's mind by the way in which the story is written. But how is this done?

Apportionment of information

As we have already seen, the difference between mystery and suspense is that in mystery a character (the villain) knows what the reader does not, whereas in suspense the reader knows what a character (the hero) does not.

For example, let's say the villain has set a trap for the hero. The audience knows this and wants to warn the hero. But they can't. Communication between the characters in a story and the readers of that story is strictly one-way. But they wish they *could* help the hero. So there you have suspense.

On the other hand, suppose some one has been killed and a cryptic message has been left behind by the killer. The killer knows what the message means. The reader does not (usually) and neither (at first) does the hero. That is an example of mystery.

This illustrates an important aspect of mystery and suspense writing in general: the apportionment of information. How the writer shares information between the characters and the readers, or between different characters, very much defines the novel being written. It is even possible to combine mystery and suspense, although it can be quite complicated.

The main tool set for dividing knowledge is the author's viewpoint.

Author's viewpoint

Broadly speaking stories can be written from any of four viewpoints:

- First person
- Third person subjective
- Author omniscient
- Third person objective

First Person

When a story is told in the first person it means that the author is addressing the reader as if he is someone involved in the story. This does not have to be the main character or even a major character, just some one who features in some way, however passively, in the story, telling the reader what he sees, what he hears, what he knows and what he thinks.

If the story is to be a mystery story, it is better if the first person narrator is *not* the detective. The reason for this is that to tell the story in the first person while withholding the narrator's thoughts is "cheating". When a story is told in the first person, the author/narrator is supposed to share not only what he sees and hears but also his *interpretation* he places on the evidence of his senses.

One of the most common and effective devices to use in such stories, is to make the narrator the hero's *sidekick*. This avoids the tricky problem of not giving away the solution without cheating, because the sidekick never knows the answer until the detective gives it. On the other hand he sees everything that the detective sees: he just doesn't know how to interpret it correctly. Let's consider the denouement to an imaginary classic British-style whodunit:

> "But surely he couldn't have got away down the corridor so quickly," I said, unable to conceal my skepticism. "Mrs Caruthers said she ran over to the window as soon as she heard the shot. And the colonel saw him walking up the staircase at the same time he

> heard the window open in Mrs Caruthers' room."
>
> It was then I noticed Lord Fortescue opening and closing the music box with that cherubic twinkle in his eyes… and I knew that he had spotted something vital that I had plainly missed.
>
> "I will explain how it was done, Jenkins," he said, in a tone that sounded mocking yet reassuring. It was as if he were trying to say: *don't worry, there's a perfectly logical explanation.*

In this well established technique, the sidekick becomes the voice of the reader, asking the detective the very questions that the reader would like to ask — challenging the detective to explain the solution piece by piece and to clarify the confusing details. This is true not only of thrillers. For example, *The Great Gatsby* is narrated by Nick Carraway, a close friend of Jay Gatsby.

In some cases it would be perfectly reasonable to make the *hero* himself/herself the narrator. He or she would describe the threat or danger or problem, what they are trying to do to negate the danger or solve the problem and the obstacles they face. However this would obviously not work if the principle danger is to the narrator himself or herself. This is because the reader would know that if the narrator is telling the story then they obviously must have survived. (In fact this is not always true. The film *Sunset Boulevard* used the unusual technique of having a voice over of a narrator who was actually dead when the film started and the story was then told in flashback. It is possible to pull this off in a novel, but probably rather hard and certainly not something that I would encourage unless you are very sure you know what you're doing.)

Yet another way to tell the story is by making the narrator a *minor* character who barely interacts with the other characters who is nevertheless present when the crucial events occur and capable of rendering an intelligent, or at least interesting, opinion. Such a narrator is very often a keen observer of human behavior and thus a fascinating voice to hear. A well-written story using this viewpoint will have the reader hanging on to the narrator's every word. This type of first person viewpoint is to some extent a variant of the third person objective or even the author omniscient as we shall see in due course. It's strength is that it allows the writer to tantalize the reader with both facts and opinions without giving too much away on the one hand, or unfairly withholding information on the other.

The great strength of the first person method is that it involves the reader with a character at the most intimate level. The reader is invited to see the story through the eyes of a real person and not a disembodied third-person author who is removed from his story.

Third person subjective

This is basically the third person equivalent of the first person. In the third person subjective, the author follows one character (the Point of View or POV character), describing them in the third person, but telling the reader their thoughts when appropriate – just as the first-person narrator might disclose his/her own thoughts. Other people's thoughts can also be presented – but only as the *speculations* of the POV character.

Consider the passage above written in the first person. Now let's see how that same passage above might be rewritten in the third person subjective.

> "But surely he couldn't have got away down the corridor so quickly," said Jenkins, unable to conceal his skepticism. "Mrs Caruthers said she ran over to the window as soon as she heard the shot. And the colonel saw him walking up the staircase at the same time he heard the window open in Mrs Caruthers' room."

> It was then that Jenkins noticed Lord Fortescue opening and closing the music box with that cherubic twinkle in his eyes… and he knew that Fortescue had spotted something vital that Jenkins himself had plainly missed.

"I will explain how it was done, Jenkins,"
said Fortescue in a tone that sounded
mocking yet reassuring. To Jenkins it was as
if he were trying to say: *don't worry, there's
a perfectly logical explanation.*

Note that in the former version, Jenkins (the narrator) shares his
thoughts with the readers and *speculates* on what Lord Fortescue is
thinking. He attributes a certain sub-text to Fortescue's tone (*don't
worry, there's a perfectly logical explanation*), but this is the first-
person narrator's *assessment* of what Fortescue is trying to say by
his tone.

In contrast, in the third-person subjective version, only Jenkins's
thoughts are related directly to the reader. When we get to Jenkins's
assessment of what is going on in Lord Fortescue's mind, this is
prefixed by the words "To Jenkins". In other words NOT: **to me the
AUTHOR "It was as if he were trying to say…"** But rather: **to
Jenkins the *character* "It was as if he were trying to say…"**

Or, in yet *other* words, the author is saying: "I – the author – haven't
a clue what Lord Fortescue was thinking, but Jenkins fancied that *he*
did." When Jenkins was himself the *first person* narrator, this
problem did not arise.

It is important to bear in mind that when writing a story from the
third-person subjective viewpoint, one does not have to stick with
the same character throughout the entire story. It is possible to write
different chapters or even different sections *within* a chapter from
different viewpoints. But one shouldn't jump around freely between
different viewpoints unless one is specifically trying to write the
story from the *author omniscient* viewpoint. (See below.)

A further point to consider here is the *number* of different characters
whose viewpoints may be used in telling the story. A guiding
principle is that it shouldn't be more than necessary. That might
sound fairly obvious but it is easily forgotten when the writer gets
the urge to indulge in flights of fancy.

Perhaps a useful thing to consider is what are the relevant events of
the story and in whose presence will they happening. Obviously if an

event occurs outside the presence of a particular character then you cannot tell it from that characters point of view, unless you wish to hold back the information in which the character learns about the event later. But in some cases you may not want to do that. Relating an event "as it happens" produces a different atmosphere to having the same event told to another character later on. Aside from the power of contemporaneous reporting, there is also greater strength in an author narrating an event and a character telling the facts to another in dialogue.

The general rule is, use as many viewpoints as you need to ensure that all the events are related to the reader, while keeping the thoughts of the villain out of the picture — at least if it is a mystery. It is not actually a hard and fast rule to keep the villain's thoughts out of it. In at least two Agatha Christie mysteries, the murderer was *the narrator*! However this too goes under the heading of "Dangerous business! To be undertaken at the author's own risk!"

There is also another circumstance in which it is possible to describe the villain's thoughts, and that is when the villain is an anonymous figure. In *Towards Zero*, Agatha Christie described the anonymous villain hatching the dastardly scheme and then proceeded to tell the rest of the story, giving the reader no inkling — until the denouement — who the villain was.

Author omniscient

In the author omniscient viewpoint the writer is the all-knowing "eye in the sky" who can not only see all the events but also read all the character's minds. To see how the author omniscient viewpoint differs from the third person subjective, let us consider how the above passage might be rewritten again, this time to make it an author-omniscient narrative.

> "But surely he couldn't have got away down the corridor so quickly," said Jenkins. He was skeptical and quite unable to conceal the fact. "Mrs Caruthers said she ran over to the window as soon as she heard the shot. And the colonel saw him walking up the staircase

at the same time he heard the window open in Mrs Caruthers' room."

By this stage Lord Fortescue was opening and closing the music box with a cherubic twinkle in his eyes. For he had spotted something vital that Jenkins had missed and he now delighted in teasing his friend with this fact. Jenkins noticed what Fortescue was doing and sensed that he was about to be ridiculed for overlooking the obvious.

"I will explain how it was done, Jenkins," said Fortescue mocking his friend but also reassuring him. The tone was Fortescue's way of telling Jenkins: *don't worry, there's a perfectly logical explanation.*

The execution is perhaps a little clumsy in my effort to differentiate this version from the third person subjective. But as you can see, from the author omniscient viewpoint the writer is free to describe the thoughts of more than one character in the same passage.

This is in some ways the most powerful viewpoint, but in others ways the weakest. It gives the author the power to describe anything and everything. But it also carries with it the problem of *holding back information* that the author does not yet want to reveal, without alerting the reader's suspicion. It is perfectly reasonable for the omniscient author to keep the story away from certain places and certain times. But on the other hand if the story is *already in a certain place at a certain time* it is not so easy to conceal people's thoughts without it clashing with the chosen style.

Suppose the author has been following the thoughts of a character who the reader is not supposed to know is the murderer. Then suddenly, at what seems like a critical juncture, the author falls silent on this matter. That is bound to jar the reader's senses and alert the reader to the fact that something is up. This is the hidden sensitive payload that the author omniscient viewpoint carries in its baggage hold. It is very hard to conceal thoughts that might give the game away without it seeming unnatural.

Of course the writer is not *obliged* to share particular thoughts with the reader, and even when he is sharing thoughts freely, they are but a fraction of all the thoughts passing through the minds of the various characters. But there must be some consistency in the style or else the reader will sense that the writer is holding out on him. This will either irritate the reader (spoiling his enjoyment of the story) or alert him to what is being hidden (destroying the mystery).

If the writer wishes to share the thoughts of various characters with the reader without giving away too much on the one hand or seeming to have gone suspiciously silent on the other, then perhaps a better viewpoint to employ is the third person *subjective* (see above) where you have more choice over whose thoughts to describe at all. By keeping the criminal's thoughts out of the picture, you avoid the big dilemma. On the other hand, people familiar with your style will soon learn to eliminate person's whose thoughts are described from the suspect list. Then again you could always vary your style from book to book or throw a googly once in a while!

If the writer were using the third person subjective viewpoint and then abruptly lapsed into the omniscient, it wouldn't necessarily give anything away, but it would jar the reader while serving no useful purpose. By and large anything that can be said as author omniscient can also be said, with a bit of enterprising refinement, in the third person subjective. But if you want to use the omniscient for its all-embracing sweep and power and if you are ready for the responsibility that goes with wielding such power, then by all means use the omniscient viewpoint.

Third person objective

This is sometimes called the journalist's voice in literature and indeed it was a style much favored by journalists who turned to writing novels, like Ernest Hemingway. In this viewpoint the writer does not describe the thoughts of *any* of the characters, but only what they do and say. On the other hand – unlike the first person or the one-viewpoint version of the third-person subjective – the author is free to follow the characters about at will and is not physically or geographically tied to one.

80

The third-person objective viewpoint has been described as turning the writer into a literary camera – a recording device for events, free to focus on anything and everything in anything from panoramic long-shot or extreme close-up, but not to penetrate the soul of psyché of the story's characters. This is a fair assessment. Indeed if a screenplay for a film were "novelised" by simply turning the present tense into the past and putting the dialogue into quotation marks, the result would be a very short novel in the third person objective viewpoint.

So how then would the passage above read if it were written from the third-person objective viewpoint?

> "But surely he couldn't have got away down the corridor so quickly," said Jenkins in a skeptical tone. "Mrs Caruthers said she ran over to the window as soon as she heard the shot. And the colonel saw him walking up the staircase at the same time he heard the window open in Mrs Caruthers' room."

> Jenkins was looking at Lord Fortescue as the aristocrat opened and closed the music box with a cherubic twinkle in his eye. Jenkins's face lit up, as if struck by the light of dawn, except that his expression still bore traces of puzzlement.

> "I will explain how it was done, Jenkins," said Fortescue mockingly, yet in a tone that was also reassuring. "You may be surprised to learn that there *is* a logical explanation."

Note that in this version we are no longer told that Jenkins realised that he had missed something. Instead we have his face being "*as if* struck by the light of dawn" but still bearing "traces of puzzlement." This is the objective way of telling the reader that Jenkins has realized something, but still not figured it out entirely. In other words he knows he has missed *something* but doesn't know *what*.

Note also that Jenkins is no longer "unable to conceal his skepticism," he merely speaks in "in a skeptical tone." Likewise Jenkins doesn't "notice" that Fortescue is "opening and closing the

81

music box with a cherubic twinkle in his eyes." He was merely "looking" at him while it happened and thus could not fail to notice it.

Another thing to note is that although this is an *objective* voice, it does not mean that it cannot contain adjectives, adjectival phrases and adverbs. Jenkins still speaks in a *skeptical* tone. Fortescue has a *cherubic twinkle* in his eyes. Jenkins face is struck by the *light of dawn* but still bears *traces of puzzlement*. Fortescue speaks *mockingly* but his tone is still *reassuring*.

Of course one wants, one can take it a stage further and cut out most of the adjectives and adverbs, making for a really terse and abrupt narrative. Such a style might seem a bit dry and uninspiring. But if the story has a lot action or even a mixture of action and dialogue then it can be quite effective as there is little in the way of psychological probing to slow down the action. Certainly this style can be used effectively in the hard-boiled genre or the *roman noire* in which the protagonist is an anti-hero. While I personally am not a fan of that genre, it is a legitimate genre and has a dedicated following.

Even if one does not seek to go to that extreme, it pays to watch the number of adjectives and adverbs, making sure not to overuse them. Descriptive words and phrases are very easy to throw in casually without much thought and they can take the form of barely-concealed padding. You may find on re-reading your manuscript that it is running much more slowly than when you wrote, when if anything it should run much quicker. That is a sure sign that it contains some form of padding and if you are pruning it, one of the first things to watch out for and be ready to cut is the excess of adjectives and adverbs.

Changing the viewpoint

As already mentioned there is the possibility, in the third-person subjective, of changing the viewpoint between characters. It is also possible to mix first and third person between different chapters or sections. Paul Erdman's *The Crash of '79* – a financial/political/military/spy thriller – used this technique to good effect. The story outlines the sequence of events resulting from a combination of the OPEC oil price increases and attempts by the Shah of Iran to dominate the region with the help of the Israelis.

Parts of the story are told in the first person from the point of view of an American financier probably based (loosely) on Erdman himself. But certain events, such as those involving he Shah, take place outside the first person narrator's presence but are simply two important to be glossed over. So instead Erdman resorts to the device of shifting to the third person when he describes these events. The technique works to very good effect, producing a riveting thriller that in my opinion is in no way dated, even though somewhat different events actually occurred in the region.

A simpler and far more common device is to mix different character viewpoints between different chapters or sections in the third person subjective viewpoint. For example if the story takes the form of a cat and mouse duel between a police detective and a criminal, then one could alternate between these two viewpoints in telling the story. The only time the writer would really have to make a choice is when the hero and villain come face to face. It would be more normal to tell the confrontation chapter from the detective's point of view. This is because even if the writer has shared much information about the villain with the reader, it will make the book more interesting if something has been held back for the climax. Otherwise, it will be boring for the reader when the villain fills in the detective on the details that the reader already knows.

How the different viewpoints can be used in the different genres

We have seen how the first person can be used as an effective viewpoint in the classic amateur or professional private detective story, with the detective's sidekick as the narrator. The same technique can be used in a police detective story, narrated from the point of view of the a young, inexperienced police officer as he watches his chief inspector or superintendent in action.

The first person is also used commonly in the streetwise hard-boiled detective genre. When used in this genre it is the detective himself rather than an any bumbling assistant who is the narrator. The story is told entirely through his eyes, following him around and his claws his way towards a solution in the face of beatings, police harassment and general opposition from an unsavoury collection of tough guys.

The use of the first person viewpoint in this genre not only restricts the story to a quest by one man to do the right thing (or maybe just earn his fee) it also provides for the hero to subject the reader to his witty, bitter or perhaps downright cynical views on life. These can be droll asides like "I felt about my accountant the way an Englishman feels about his mother-in-law." Or they can be descriptions of another character: "He had more faces than Mount Rushmore." If the author is looking for a derogatory physical description he might say: "He looked like the sphinx — or at least the wrong end of it."

One has to be careful not to get carried away with that sort of pseudo-tough talk. It can easily degenerate into a parody of itself, as some of those hastily-cobbled together examples no doubt show!

The third-person objective viewpoint can be used in a police procedural with a multi-plot story and a large collection of characters. There may be too many people to select the right two or three to use as viewpoint characters. Instead the writer can simply follow them around like a camera, reporting what they say and do.

The same technique could be used in a techno-thriller. When some scientific or technological detail needs to be explained to the reader, one could have a scientist or engineer explain it to a less knowledgeable character, with the ignorant party asking probing questions of the type that the reader might ask, to punctuate the scientist's explanation and thus avoid having a large block of speech put into one man's mouth uninterrupted.

The third person subjective can be used in a woman-in-jeopardy story told from a single viewpoint to get the reader to identify with the heroine while at the same time not trying to force the reader to view her completely from within. This might be the preferred option for a male author writing a woman in jeopardy story.

A political thriller could be written as a multi-viewpoint third person narrative, showing the nefarious activities of some and the idealistic efforts of others to stop them.

These are of course merely suggestions and examples. There is no absolute requirement that a hard-boiled detective story *must* be written in the first person or that a techno-thriller must be written as a third person objective story. It is up to the writer to find the way that suits his or her purpose. And remember that the hardest part of being a writer is to find something new to say or a new way of saying something.

Chapter 5 - How to describe things, people and places

The descriptive voice in essence

We have already noted that a story is about things being *done*. It is about *events*. It may contain dialogue as well as action — most stories usually do. But it must be about events, occurrences and actions. The essence of a story is *change*. It cannot stay at the same place the whole time – unless it is a mood piece. It may *end up* where it started, but it must *travel to get there* — like a hand sweeping round a clock face, to those who still remember analogue clocks and watches!

In the case of a thriller it is unlikely even to end up where it started and will certainly not be a mood piece. Mood pieces tend to hover on the same spot like a helicopter. A thriller must move – usually forward, sometimes backward. It's raison d'etre is *change*. Thus thrillers will have a lot of narrative and a fair amount of dialogue, the precise proportions depending on the plot and the genre.

It might therefore seem strange to discuss descriptive writing before looking at narrative and dialogue. However, it is important to remember that in fiction, as in life, nothing beats actually being there. And the purpose of descriptive writing is to give the reader that sense of being there.

The experience of a work of fiction is greatly enhanced for the audience if get to share the sensory input that the characters are experiencing. The thrill of a legal trial, for example, is actually to be there in that courtroom when the lawyer exposes the conspiracy. The thrill of a police procedural is to be there in that police station, when the suspect finally confesses and tells them where he buried the murder weapon. The thrill of an action adventure or spy thriller is to be running along with James Bond as he springs along the gangway to get to the master switch of the mechanism that Bloefeld is planning on using to destroy the world!

In the case of a movie, the writer – working closely with the director, actors and a host of others – can take the audience to the time and place visually and aurally. But in the case of a book, we do not have the power of moving pictures on a wide screen or a six channel Dolby sound system. *All we have are our words.* Fortunately, this means that. *if we get it right*, we can do what we do it on a much lower budget than Hollywood! Furthermore, we can give the reader something that the viewer doesn't get in the cinema. We can give our audience not just the sight and sound of the action but also the smell of the place, the taste of the food and *the feelings of the hero* — or of the villain, if we are of a mind to do so.

The importance of descriptive writing then is that it enables us to take our readers and draw them into our story by giving them a sense of presence: by making them feel as if they are actually there.

The descriptive voice is the author's voice – sometimes a character's voice – telling the reader about people, places, objects and even the abstract atmosphere in a given situation. It is a voice that contains, adjectives and adverbs. But it can also be used to advance the story as well as evoke the current time and place. Furthermore, one does not necessarily have to use the *descriptive voice* alone, in order to convey a *description* as such. You can convey a description through a narrative voice. We shall see this more clearly later.

The descriptive voice as a tool of characterization

Describing people

One of the most obvious uses of the descriptive voice is to introduce the reader to *people*, to the characters in the story. As an example, let's take this description of a character from Ruth Rendell's *The Keys to the Street*.

> The name everyone called him was Hob, the three letters of which were the initials of his two given names and his surname. Apart from this, the feature that distinguished him from his contemporaries was the size of his head. His body was solid and thickset but his

head still looked too big for it. When he reached fifty, if he ever did, his jowls would be down on his shoulders. His fair hair was cut an inch long all over his big head and gleamed in the yellowish chemical light. It was an unusual combination, that of fair hair and brown eyes. His eyes were a curious textured brown, like chocolate mousse, and the pupils were sometimes as big as a cat's and sometimes the size of a full stop on a keyboard.

Note that this is a very *physical* description. It does not contain much by way of *opinion*, only a selection of illustrative *facts*. The description does not tell us whether the character is good-looking or ugly, it merely gives us factual information that permits us to make up our own minds. We are told that the body is "solid and thickset" and that the head is "too big" for the body. The words "too big for" might be construed as the author's opinion, but it is still an opinion stated in the form of a fact.

In general, a factual description will usually contain a subjective element, while purporting to deliver an objective *conclusion*. It might be thought of as a kind of *objective* letter inside a *subjective* envelope. To understand the difference, consider this illustration. Supposing we were talking instead about something abstract like a character's intelligence. Let's look at three statements that might describe this characteristic:

1. "He was extremely intelligent – a real genius in fact."

2. "He was a patent attorney with a first class honors Juris Doctor degree from Harvard and an BS in chemistry, summa cum laude from Princeton. As a practitioner before the World Intellectual Property Organization, he was also fluent in French and German."

3. "At school he always stood out head and shoulders above the other students, getting straight A's without appearing to make any real effort."

In the first example, the writer is offering an opinion, pure and simple. It may very well be true, but we are being asked to accept the author's uncorroborated assertion. There is no room for the reader to think about the issue independently. Either the reader believes the author or he doesn't. Of course in practice the reader will usually accept the author's assertions about his own characters, but at a price. While accepting the intelligence of this character as a fact, the reader will form a very *personal* opinion of what *form* that intelligence takes. If the reader's own idea of intelligence or genius is possessing a lot of trivial general knowledge then this is what he will expect of the character. If, on the other hand, the reader associates intelligence with being a brilliant specialist in some demanding intellectual discipline and if the character then does not live up to these expectations, then that particular reader will be disappointed.

Likewise, if the writer says that the character has "good judgment" but proceeds to narrate a sequence of events in which the character demonstrates *bad* judgment, then the narrative will clash with the reader's expectations, leaving the reader not surprised but simply frustrated.

In the second example above, the writer gives us a purely *factual* statement. In straightforward, no-nonsense fashion the writer tells us straight out about the character's profession, his academic qualifications and the highly respected universities from which he obtained them. Much of the impact of this description will come from the large gulf between these two qualifications. The degrees are in entirely different fields, one legal, the other scientific. Furthermore, the character obtained them from two very eminent institutions. Finally, the description is rounded off by a reference to his linguistic skills. This does not imply, however, that he is more than just a "jack of all trades but a master of none." Rather it suggests that he is a twentieth century renaissance man and polymath, with a diverse range of expertise.

"Ah," the reader will say, on reading this description. "Now *that's* an intelligent man."

The writer will thus plant the idea of the character's intelligence in the reader's mind without even *using* the word "intelligent".

In the third example, however, we see a combination of the objective and the subjective. We are told that he "stood out head and shoulders above the other students…" but not told what sort of grades the others got. Of course, the fact that it says *head and shoulders* above the other students" suggests that he didn't just get A- or B+ grades, as that would not be a "head and shoulders" disparity. However, it is not stated in unambiguous factual form. That he stood out above the other students is either a fact or a lie — in that sense it is an *objective* statement. But whether the disparity was sufficient to justify the words "head and shoulders" is a matter on which opinions might differ. Even if an impartial observer familiar with the facts were to disagree, it doesn't make it a lie. In that sense it is a *subjective* statement — a value judgment.

This pattern is repeated in the rest of the description. We are told that he got "straight A grades" but not told how high the standard of the school was. We could, if we wanted to be petty, speculate that perhaps the school had a low standard and that his high grades did not signify true intelligence. Finally we are told that he didn't *appear* to make any real effort, but it is made clear that this is merely how it *looked to others*. He might in fact have been making a very great effort.

Such combined objective-subjective descriptions do not usually strain the credulity of the reader, as long as the overall characterization is consistent. Virtually all readers will conclude on a basis of the third description that the character is intelligent, just as they probably would from the other two. Of course they *could* engage in petty quibbling in their own minds. But in practice they will simply accept that the man is intelligent and will carry on reading with this belief in mind.

The third description is in many ways the most approachable to the average reader. It avoids the pitfalls of the purely subjective author's opinion, while at the same time gently prodding the reader's thoughts in the direction the writer wants them to go. The writer does not count on the reader knowing about the high academic standards of Oxford or Imperial College, nor rely on them to ponder the intellectual implications of a person having academic qualifications in such diverse disciplines as chemistry and law.

However, all three descriptive methods are valid, depending on what the author is trying to achieve. It is up to the author to select the approach that is most suitable for the story (and character) in question.

Going back to Rendell's description of Hob, another interesting feature of it is that it discusses not only his looks, but also his lifestyle. Here again, Rendell does not pass value judgment (or moral judgment) on what she is writing about, but does let us know, by way of a hint, that it is a lifestyle not altogether conducive to longevity ("When he reached fifty, *if he ever did…*").

As in the second and third descriptions of our characters intelligence in the examples above, this is an important example of that time-honored writer's dictum: show, don't tell. The reference to Hob's lifestyle is like the third example above: the objective missive enclosed in the subjective envelope. At that stage in the novel, Rendell has yet to tell us what Hob's lifestyle is, but she prepares us for it with an ominous statement about his survival prospects.

Returning to Hob's *physical* appearance, as descriptions go, this is quite a detailed one. It provides us with a very clear picture of the characters natural attributes. This is interesting, inasmuch as it helps us to picture the character and thus have a sense of being there with him in the events of the story in which he takes part. But it does not tell us what sort of a person the character is, as his natural looks are only a limited indicator of his lifestyle.

Describing clothing

There is however another aspect of a person's appearance that gives us far more information about a character's nature. That is, of course, the way he or she dresses. A person has only limited control over his body shape and even less over his face (although Abraham

Lincoln is reputed to have said on one occasion that "any man over 40 is responsible for his face"). But we can certainly choose the way we dress. Indeed amongst the young, dressing in a particular way to make a statement about oneself is par for the course.

With older people it is perhaps less a conscious statement than an expression of their practical circumstances. If a man works in an office (or as a salesman in a department store), he probably has to wear a suit. A factory worker in light industry may wear casual clothes. In heavy industry, while at work, he may wear protective overalls or a boiler suit. A trial lawyer in a British court (think "Rumpole of the Bailey") will wear robes. An American lawyer will wear a suit. A policeman will wear a uniform, unless he is a detective in which case he will wear ordinary street clothes. If he is infiltrating a rock festival to catch drug pushers he may sport a beard and wear a T-shirt and jeans (who knows, he may even come to like the hippie lifestyle and decide to quit life's rat race!).

Even off duty, a person's clothing may reflect their work as well as their socio-economic background. Take this descriptive passage from *The Big Byte* by Peter J Ognibene.

> Though medals and epaulets were nowhere to be seen, Otis Wheeler's three-piece wool suit was poor camouflage: the man was unmistakably a military officer. Erect in bearing, though a bit too short for a recruiting poster, Wheeler had wavy blond hair that was graying at the fringes, a strong straight nose, and a steady gaze. A blue-eyed eagle.

In this description we see again the facts and the opinions cleverly intermingled. On the factual level we have a "three-piece wool suit," "wavy blond hair… graying at the fringes," "a strong straight nose" and "erect in bearing." Although the description is in the third-person *subjective* viewpoint (viewpoints will be covered later), these are all raw *facts*. We even have the negative "fact" of an *absence* of "medals and epaulets." On the opinion level — not of the author, but of the character who was watching Wheeler — we learn that the suit was "poor camouflage" and that Wheeler is "unmistakably a military officer." But this is qualified by the opinion that he was "a bit too short for a recruiting officer."

Sub-text to a description

The reference to Wheeler's height serves a more subtle purpose than merely filling out the physical picture of the man. The choice of words "too short for a recruiting poster" is by no means accidental. It is designed to tell us, at the subconscious level, a little bit more about the man. He is a military officer, yes, but he is not *100%* military. There is an element of independence about him… maybe even an element of the *civilian*. In the story he does in fact try to play a conciliatory role between the character who is looking at him (a man of liberal political convictions) and a government intelligence agency.

Thus the physical description, by qualifying his military image, prepares us to accept his subsequent characterization as a *military diplomat*. He is a man whose life is squarely in one camp (the military) but who understands and speaks the language of another (civilians). This characterization is accomplished later in the book by a lot more than a mere physical description. It is disclosed mainly through the dialogue. But the description is consistent with the image that the author is trying to create and it seamlessly blends in with the rest of the characterization as it develops further in the book. This gives the writing the virtue of *consistency*.

The length of a description, and the amount of detail one goes into when writing descriptively, obviously varies according to the importance of the character in the story. A major character, whom we are going to follow throughout the story, merits a longer description (not necessarily in a single passage). A minor character, might be treated with a brief description or even no description at all. Indeed, a brief description might be worked into the story in a fraction of a sentence, barely registering as description on the reader's consciousness, but nevertheless planting a visual image in the reader's mind. An example of this is a brief descriptive line from Jeffrey Archer's *Shall We Tell the President*.

> Senator Thornton of Texas, thin and gaunt
> with greasy black hair, whom Mark
> remembered from Mr Smith's Restaurant,
> had only just begun to…

Note how the sentence doesn't even stop to let the description sink in. It rolls on relentlessly with the action. But this does not mean that the description is forgotten. Even though we do not dwell on it in our minds, we subconsciously take in the adjectives like "thin", "gaunt" and "greasy" - forming a picture in our minds as the action progresses.

A description can convey information not only about the person being described, but also about another person who is interacting with them. This is especially true in passages written from third person objective or first person viewpoints. The following example is also from Peter J Ognibene's *The Big Byte*. Before reading it, bear in mind the following points:

a) The hero is a happily married man (with no children), who has been persuaded (reluctantly) to work with the government on a matter of national security.

b) An attempt has been made on his life and the government have convinced him that the best way to protect him and his wife is to make it seem as if he is dead and not to tell anyone that he is alive who doesn't actually need to know – not even his wife!

Now, with that in mind, read this description of the woman who heads the defense contractor and consultancy *that he will soon be working with* on this government sponsored mission.

> She moved like a dancer, and Paul's eye
> fixed on her from a distance when all he
> could see was the outline of a tall brunette
> walking towards him. There was both grace
> and precision to her step, elegant symmetry
> as each foot was splayed and extended
> forward.

As you can see from this brief description and the context, there is a lot going on here. At one level we are learning what a major

94

character in the story looks like, so that as the story progresses, with her in it, we are able to picture her in our mind's eye. But at another level we learn an immense amount about the man from who's point of view the description is given in this *third-person subjective* viewpoint. Here is a man who *loves his wife*, but who is removed from her and *denied contact with her* by the current circumstances, finding himself in a *situation of loneliness* where he is subjected to the first hint of *temptation*. Thus while the description is telling us explicitly about the woman's *body*, it is telling us implicitly about the man's *mind*.

In the first chapter of my first thriller, *A Fool for a Client*, there is a scene in the judge's chambers in which he begins to develop protective feelings towards the female defendant. I approached this by way of a physical description of the girl through the judge's eyes, leading up to an explicit statement of his feelings.

> Half a minute ticked by while the judge stared at Justine. Her height was only a few inches above average, but he could see immediately the enormous power pent up within her. Most women would have regarded her as slightly overweight, but to men she was a Grecian goddess, cast from the same mold as the classic statues. Even from afar one could see the straight, broad back of a rock climber, the powerful shoulders of a swimmer and the long, well-toned but not muscular legs of a runner. But her image could never have been preserved in marble or bronze. For Justine Levy had the quality of something firm yet constantly in motion. Only kinetic sculpture could have captured her essence. She was a robot with a face of ivory and a body of tempered steel.

> Apart from her smooth complexion, her eyes were nature's major concession to her femininity. They were wide, inset deeply in large orbits, looking out at the world like the trusting curious eyes of a child until a change of mood made them narrow down into feline

> slits that neither sought nor offered
> comfort…
>
> …*be careful*, he told himself. *Don't get
> involved…*

Only after reading how the judge sees Justine do we read an explicit statement about his feelings for her. But by then we have already got a *sense* that he is attracted to her, even though it is equally clear that not everyone would find her physically attractive.

Where the description is given from the first person viewpoint, one can bring in the character's thoughts directly, right there along with the description, with far less preamble. A good, brief example of this is provided by Denise Danks in *Frame Grabber*.

> He looked young, thirty-eight, smooth-faced
> and fair. His eyes were like the sky, blue,
> and, yes, all over me.

Such first person descriptive writing can of course help to define the relationships between characters. By that I mean not just the formal relationship, but the attitudes of one towards the other. Michael Ridpath's *Free to Trade* provides another good example.

> Behind this rush of energy came Cathy. She
> was tall and walked into the room with an
> awkward angular grace. Her dark hair was
> tied tightly back behind her neck. She wore a
> crisp white blouse under an expensive
> looking blue suit, with a delicate set of small
> pearl earrings. She had a figure designed to
> wear elegant clothes, slim with sharp edges.
> But I couldn't help noticing her eyes; large
> and brown, they carefully avoided contact
> with anyone in the room. I could see what
> Rob meant. She had a mixture of
> untouchable beauty and vulnerability that
> must have been giving him all sorts of
> problems.

In this passage we learn about Cathy, about the narrator's friend Rob and about the narrator himself. Of course we learn mainly about

Cathy, but we get a sense of what is going through Rob's mind and an insight into the friendship between Rob and the narrator.

Using the descriptive voice to set the stage

Describing places in the story

As with descriptions of people, describing *places* serves several purposes. At one level it simply gives the readers that sense of being there that holds the their attention and makes them feel part of the story, making them want to read on. At another level it can set the stage for places that play an important part in the story, provide a background for introducing major characters in their natural habitat or simply stimulate at emotion in the reader comparable to the emotion that the place itself would trigger in a first time visitor — although perhaps with not quite the same intensity.

Let's take another passage from Ruth Rendell's *The Keys to the Street* this time a description of Regent's Park.

> The Park is deserted by night. That is, the intention is that it should be deserted. The Park Police patrol between dusk and dawn, paying special attention to the restaurant areas that make likely shelters and to the park residences, the villas, the expensive properties and Winfield House where the American ambassador lives. No vagrant could sleep undisturbed under the lee of the pavilions or the bandstand, but the police cannot search everywhere every night. The canal bank remains a place of concealment and the wide green spaces and, in summer, the long grass under the trees.

This is just part of a long description that conjures up images and truly evokes the Park. Note that as with her description of "Hob" above, this is a very fact-oriented description. She doesn't tell us that the park is "lovely" or "vast" or "a joy to visit". Now on the other hand that it is "cold" or "frightening" or "mysterious". She tells us factual details that build up a picture in the minds of readers who have never been there, so that they will feel as if they have. As one who has been to Regent's Park many times, both as a child and as an adult, I can testify to the authenticity of her description.

As a general rule one should watch the length of description's very carefully, both as regards the length of a particular descriptive passage and as regards the overall amount of space devoted to describing a particular place, otherwise it can get in the way of the story. As with descriptions of people, the writer has more scope for long descriptions if the story is being told in the first person, because then the readers find themselves swept along with the thoughts of the person whose mind they are sharing. Here is a passage from another book by Michael Ridpath called *Trading Reality*.

> I turned back towards Kirkhaven, a crowded little town of pale houses, crammed together on the hillside. The muffled sounds of the sea soon became a lulling, soothing background to the odd cry of seagulls. Every now and then I could hear an old car engine straining to negotiate the narrow winding streets and steep hills of the town. Three church towers rose proudly above the houses; not for nothing was it called Kirkhaven. To the left of the harbour front, I saw the mouth of the Inch, winding its way through rocks and sand between my brother's house and the graveyard of the church opposite. Daffodils lined the bank.

The length of the and detail description is justified not only by the first-person viewpoint, but also by the fact that the narrator's brother has been killed and this their childhood haunt, where he is going to bury his brother.

Important places

Places that feature prominently in a story are entitled to a longer description than places which are of merely — excuse the pun — passing interest. Take Brad Meltzer's *The Tenth Justice* a thriller involving a young law graduate who has just started his legal internship with a judge of the United States Supreme Court.

> As he stood outside the Supreme Court, a half-hour early for his first day on the job, he was entranced by the gleaming white columns of the nation's highest court. This is it, he thought, taking a deep breath. It's finally here. Running his hand through his recently cut brown hair, Ben climbed the wide marble stairs. He counted each step, in case Justice Hollis was curious how many stairs there were. Forty-four, he told himself, filing the information on a mental index card.

A "mental card index" might be an anachronism in the age of the tablet and smart phone, but putting that aside, let's take a closer look at the description. Firstly, note how it devotes only a few words to the physical features like "gleaming white columns" and "wide marble steps." But around that physical description is an insight into the protagonist's nervousness as he prepares to start his first day at work there. Once again we see this dualistic character – so often found in descriptive passages – of the description of one entity (in this case a place) being used as a vehicle to clue us in to the thoughts of another entity (i. e. the hero of the story). Many descriptions written from the first person or third person subjective viewpoints are external descriptions of one entity and internal descriptions of another.

In the passage above we were introduced not only to a main venue that features prominently in the story, but also to the hero of the story. When introducing characters, especially major characters, attention should always be paid to *where* they are introduced. It might be where they work, or where they live, or where they play. In the example above, the hero was introduced arriving at the place where he was going to start working — a place which was to be the local point of a story about the struggle for justice against a dishonest shadowy figure in the background.

Applying this principle in general can yield some interesting dilemmas. A tough private eye in a story of the hard-boiled genre might be introduced to the reader in his dilapidated office looking through a pile of bills that he cannot pay due to lack of clients. Alternatively, he could be introduced at his favorite bar where he has gone to drown his sorrows in Tennessee's finest!

The classic example is the story about a mother's struggle for revenge/justice after her child is knocked down by a drunk driver. Do you introduce the mother at the gates of the school, dropping off or picking up her other child? Or do you introduce her at her place of work where she hears the bad news? Then again, perhaps you introduce her when she is cleaning the child's room, not realizing the news she is about to receive?

Everyone of these approaches is valid and each serves a different purpose and stands to create a different mood and atmosphere. There is no overall right answer. The right answer depends what you the writer are trying to achieve. Does the tragedy make the mother over-protective towards her other child? Does it make her quit her job to spend more time with the other child (or more time on her quest for justice). Or does she later turn the room into a shrine for her dead child, a symbol of her obsession with her loss that sets the stage for her subsequent pursuit of revenge?

In *The Silence of the Lambs*, Thomas Harris – writing in the present tense – introduces the evil but brilliant psychiatrist-turned-serial-murderer, Hannibal Lecter, in the cell in a psychiatric hospital where he is now detained.

> Dr Lecter's cell is well beyond the others, facing only a closet across the corridor, and it is unique in other ways. The front is a wall of bars, but within the bars, at a distance greater than the human reach, is a second barrier, a stout nylon net, stretched from floor to ceiling and wall to wall. Behind the net, Starling could see a table bolted to the floor and piled high with softcover books and papers and a straight chair, also fastened down.

The value of carefully selecting a place where a major character is to be introduced should not be under-rated.

Advancing the story

In addition to assisting in characterization or setting the scene for future developments, description can also be used to advance the plot itself. A common example of this might occur when some one is found dead. Such an occurrence is quite likely to be a major turning point in the story. so it makes perfect sense to describe the site as graphically as the writer's sensibilities will allow. Here is an example from Jeffrey Archer's *Shall We Tell the President?*

> Warm fresh blood was flowing over the bottom sheet, trickling from Casefikis's mouth, his dark eyes bulged from their sockets, his tongue was hanging loose and swollen. His throat had been cut ear to ear, just below the chin line. The blood was starting to make a pool on the floor. Mark was standing in it.

And here's another from Scott Turow's *Pleading Guilty.*

> It wasn't Bert. This guy was about Bert's size, but he was older, maybe sixty. He had been folded into the refrigerator like a garment bag. His feet went one way, his legs were squashed down under him, his head was forced about ninety degrees to make him fit. His eyes were bugged out unbelievably; they were that very light green you might as well call gray. He was wearing a suit and a tie, and around the collar of his shirt, the blood had soaked in and dried like a kind of batik. Eventually I noticed the black line dug into his neck and tied to a shelf hook to hold him up. Fishing tackle. Deep-sea stuff. One hundred-pound test. The refrigerator light glowed like a bald head and threw a little orange into his gray face. Alive, he must have been a respectable-looking fellow.

Clearly, from these descriptions, a major event has occurred and the story is about to move up into a higher gear.

Graphic description is a useful tool for advancing a story when you want a major event to take place outside the presence of the hero in a story written in the first person or third person subjective viewpoint. However dialogue is an equally good tool for that purpose. And neither description nor dialogue are substitutes for narrative when you are writing an author omniscient or third person objective or multi-viewpoint subjective story. On such occasions it is better to narrate the landmark event — unless of course you have some reason to hold back, such as to create a mystery as to *what* precisely happened.

Methods of description

As we have already seen there are different ways in which the descriptive voice can be used. It can present us with solid facts, the author's opinions or a character's opinions. It can be a purely descriptive voice or it can be intermingled with narrative passages. It is worth considering these differences in more detail.

Subjective description

Imagine some one writing about London and telling us what they think of it. Let's take a made up description.

> He had mixed feelings about London. It was a city of contrasts. In it innermost reaches it positively *radiated* power: the power of retail commerce, the power of international trade and the power of national politics, like three brothers who had grown up together and were now each going their own separate ways. But it was also a city of charm, a collection of little villages each with their own character. In these villages, one could find both warmth and coldness, both friendship and aloofness. And it could also be a city of gloom, of misery — a city from

which even its most fervent admirers
sometimes wanted to escape.

Now you might well agree with every word in that passage. It's not actually difficult to write an agreeable passage when one hedges ones bets so much and qualifies every assertion with a contradictory side comment. But you will notice in that passage, if you read it carefully, that it doesn't actually contain any *facts*. It is a collection of opinions without the slightest attempt to state the premises on which those opinions are based.

Yes, there are hints and clues. Those familiar with London will know about the bustling retail center of its West End. Most people will also know about the City of London, the famous Square Mile in which so much international financial trade is conducted. Likewise people know about the Houses of Parliament in Westminster and its associated civil service in Whitehall — a government apparatus that still wields considerable influence abroad as well as at home despite the erosion of its power through the fall of the empire, the rise of the United States and the encroachment of the European Union.

Similarly we can imagine the warm, friendly patter of the London taxi driver hoping for a big tip or the cold avoidance of eye-contact by the other passengers trying to fight their way onto the tube. The village character of London with its Petticoat Lane and Smithfield meat market, Chinatown in Soho and the Italian community in the Farringdon area will also be familiar to those who know London.

So the description is certainly a truthful one. But it relies heavily on the reader's existing knowledge and invites the reader to share the author's conclusion. The problem is of course that if the reader has enough knowledge of London to agree with the author's opinion, then he doesn't need the author to spell it out to him. Alternatively, if the reader has no knowledge of London, he might well accept the author's conclusions, but still be left bewildered as to what it all means in practice. It will produce in the reader some vague nebulous sense of what the author is trying to say like… like seeing a figure in the fog and not being sure if it is one's own father or not (with apologies to William Shakespeare).

103

My personal opinion is that this method of description is not good, because it fails to produce a clear picture in the reader's mind. Of course, you might say, most people *do* know something about London whether they are based in a Welsh valley, the Swiss Alps or a small town in the mid-west of the United States. And it is true, in the case of a major city like London, or Paris or New York, most readers will know a fair amount about it through television, books, newspaper articles, movies, etc. But as writers we cannot rely on this knowledge in all cases and writing sloppy, nebulous descriptions is a bad habit to get into.

Also, even if one is writing about a place that the reader is likely to be familiar with — and putting aside the "in that case why bother?" question — even familiar places change over time. The London of the year 2015 is very different to the London of 1970 (automated teller machines, huge suburban supermarkets and shopping malls, the decline of local shops, fewer sub-post-offices, the Docklands development, the Millennium Dome, the Jubilee line, not to mention its extension). And of course the London of 1960 was different still (trolley buses, cars driving into Leicester Square, fewer tall buildings, the *old* Euston station with its great arch, blue police phone boxes — hence Doctor Who's TARDIS — and of course different hairstyles!).

Objective description

One of the reasons that the books of Charles Dickens have such a timeless quality is that he went to great trouble to give his readers detailed factual descriptions of the places he was writing about. Whether it was the great Inn's of Court or the fog-haunted Thames, Dickens brought it to life with evocative, factual description. So now, even if these places have changed, we can still imagine them as they were then, as Dickens saw them.

Now, it was perhaps not *purely* out of a conscious desire for timelessness that Dickens gave such beautiful, graphic descriptions. He was well aware that many of the people in his own time had never seen these places. Travel was not so easy in those days. Although trains existed in his day, not everyone in a welsh valley or a Scots glen or an industrial town in the midlands had the means — or the need — to hop on a train to London. Not everyone could afford a day trip or weekend short-break in those days. And of course television and cinema didn't exist in those days, so views of distant places were not routinely taken into people's living rooms. So Dickens wrote detailed descriptions to introduce his locations to those were unfamiliar with them even in his own day.

But there is no denying that the *effect* of Dickens' meticulousness is to make his books intelligible and approachable today to readers who have set eyes on the London of Dickens's time. Now, this leads to a tricky question for a writer of thrillers. Because although books remain available through public libraries many years or even decades after publication, most thrillers have a fairly short shelf life, unless they are major successes or better still become classics. You can certainly buy the books of Agatha Christie online, and if you can't get them there, you can almost certainly do so at a specialist crime bookshop. But the likelihood that readers will be reading in ten or twenty years time a book that you wrote today is exceedingly small. It saddens me too (along with the equally depressing alternative that they might start reading my books after I'm dead and no longer able to collect the royalties) but it is nevertheless true.

The tricky question then is should we aim to write factual informative, objective descriptions that will stand as our memorials for posterity and will be understood by those unfamiliar with the places we're writing about? My answer is *yes*. Apart from the fact that it gives the writing greater accessibility to a broader base and gives the writing a more timeless quality, it also simply makes for *better* writing. That alone is reason enough to do it.

But the question is how objective? Here's a made-up fact oriented description.

> It's inner city streets were narrow — in contrast to the wide boulevards of Paris. On the road to his right, cars crawled along at a snail's pace. There was a blue Ford Mondeo hooting it's horn at a green Renault Cleo in front. In the Cleo sat a twenty two year old

blonde who scowled into her rear view mirror. Ahead of him in the distance was Canada Tower in Canary Wharf. Once the tallest building in London, when it overtook the Nat West building, it has now itself been bested itself by the Shard. A bright red bus passed by on the far side of the road. On its side, close to the top, was an advertisement for a new comedy film, some box-office blockbuster from Hollywood.

Unlike our earlier passage, this description has nothing *but* fact. But there are several problems with it. For a start there is no effort to *select* the facts, they are simply thrown in like leftovers into a casserole. There is no attempt to build up a *coherent* picture of something *in particular*. The facts tend to jump around at random.

Now you might say that the description is following the stream of consciousness of the character. But it doesn't really get anywhere. It consists of a series of parts that do not add up to any particular sum. If the author is trying to say something about the character who is thinking these thoughts, then what is it? That he is bored? That he has a low attention span? That he is an assiduous observer of detail with a great memory for facts? The author might mean any of these things, but he provides us with nothing to differentiate or decide which.

Okay, you might say, but maybe the author is trying to create an image of the chaos of the London rush hour. But if so why mention the various tall buildings? They are not part of the rush hour. They stand there all the time. People may be rushing to them or going home from them, but why discuss their heights and their history? What has *that* got to do with the rush hour. And why mention the precise age of the blonde? Would it matter to the scene if she was 20 or 25. Why not just say a blonde woman in her twenties?

The pitfall with objective writing is that there is no practical limit to *the number of details* or extent of minute dissection the writer can do in describing a place, or possibly even a person. If the character jumps on a bus to effect his escape or to follow some one, do you just describe the suspicious stares of the other passengers in brief?

106

Or do you describe every passenger in detail? Do you describe their facial appearances or also their bodies. Do you describe their clothes? Do you then describe what they wore yesterday. Clearly such attention to detail can rapidly degenerate into absurdity. As a writer you have to *select* just enough detail to convey the picture to your reader without going overboard with detail that the reader neither needs nor wants and that can only serve to slow down your story.

But the problem is that every reader is different and selecting just enough detail to convey the particular impression you want to convey might be hard. If you only include objective facts, you might find that you genuinely have to include a *lot* of detail in order to convey the full picture.

But what if you can get around this problem by having the best of both worlds? What if you can do what we talked about before: combine the objective with the subjective?

Objective facts and subjective conclusions

We have now got to the stage that we have really been heading for since the beginning of this chapter. A descriptive passage can be written with a few *carefully selected* facts that illustrate a place or person without dotting the I's and crossing the T's, and then *underscored* by a statement of *what the parts add up to*.

Let's take another passage from Michael Ridpath's *Trading Reality*.

> They were arrayed along the other side of the boardroom table, four Japanese in a row. Dark blue or grey suits, white shirts, wild swirling ties. The ties had intricate patterns of leaves, peacocks, bright suns. The effect was spoilt by the fact that all four were wearing them. Conformity in rebellion.

Note the factual part first: the position of the Japanese, their suits and shirts and "swirling ties". Then the statement about the effect being spoilt because they were all wearing the same tie. Then, finally the first person author's interpretation: "Conformity in rebellion."

Note also how the author splits the interpretation into two phases. First he hints at it with the words "the effect was spoilt by…" At that point we have a sense of what he means, but not a firm conviction. Only then does he underscore it with a more explicit statement: "Conformity in rebellion."

It would not have been nearly as good if he had said: "The effect of rebellion was spoilt by the conformity of each wearing the same tie." It would have conveyed the same *information*, but it would not have created the same effect. By telling it in this way he shows how the author-character himself took in this information in quick but separate stages of realization. The character is seeing these men — whose decisions will be important to him — and *assessing* them. It is a tribute to the writer's skill that he chose his words so precisely and carefully to get this subtle effect just right.

We can see another example of this approach in Scott Turow's *Pleading Guilty*.

> He's a sizable man, Martin, a wrestler at the U three decades ago, a middleweight with a chest broad as the map of America. He has a dark, shrewd face, a little like those Mongol warriors of Genghis Khan's, and the venerable look of somebody who's mixed it up with life. He is, no question, the best lawyer I know.

Here we see facts and opinions cleverly blended together. There's the adjective "sizable", the reference to his background "a wrestler" which conveys a combative spirit. Then, when we get onto his face, we find two adjectives strung together: "dark" and "shrewd". The first is objective, the second subjective. Then an opinion that enhances the fighting spirit image that the author is trying to convey: "Mongol warriors". Followed by another fact-opinion construct that shifts the emphasis from combat to maturity and, by implication, the wisdom that goes with it: "the venerable look of somebody who's mixed it up with life." At the end of all that we get the summation of the parts, telling us what these fragments of fact and opinion add up to: "the best lawyer I know."

If he had said "the best lawyer in the world," the build-up would not have been enough to convince the reader, because it did not contain sufficient raw data and indeed was at least 50% opinion. But as the final statement describes him as "the best lawyer *I know*" it works perfectly. The conclusion is itself that wonderful *objective message in subjective wrapping* that I was extolling earlier.

The same approach as was used above for *people* can be used to describe places. In Ayn Rand's pro-libertarian novel *Atlas Shrugged*, the author gives a description of New York city in the evening twilight to evoke an image of a once-great city (and by implication the national economy that went with it) in a state terminal decline.

> The clouds and the shafts of light of skyscrapers against them were turning brown, like an old painting in oil, the color of a fading masterpiece. Long streaks of grime ran from under the pinnacle down the slender, soot-eaten walls. High on the side of a tower there was a crack in the shape of a motionless lightning, the length of ten stories. A jagged object cut the sky above the roofs; it was half a spire, still holding the glow of the sunset; the gold leaf had long since peeled off the other half. The glow was red and still like the reflection of a fire: not an active fire, but a dying one which it is too late to stop.

Note the clever use of the artistic analogy "the color of a fading masterpiece" to convey in a single phrase both connotations of greatness and images of inexorable decline. The spire — a symbol of religious faith — is another clever metaphor, along with the peeling away of half the gold while the other half is still intact. This conveys the twilight state of the economy in the novel. Finally the direction in which things are heading is underlined by the ominous final pair of clauses: "not an active fire, but a dying one which it is too late to stop."

Description through narrative and use of verbs

It might be assumed that in order to describe a person or place one has to use the descriptive voice. But there is a problem with this method. When we look at a *visual* image we see all of its parts in one go. We may not take in all the detail at first glance, but it is all there right in front of us. However when we *read a description* of a person or place, we get the facts *one at a time*. It's a bit like waiting for an image to download on the internet. We sit and wait while the image scans slowly down a box from top to bottom or we start off with a very boxy, pixelated image until the details are filled out and come into focus.

This problem is inherent in the nature of words. Unlike an image, words are strung together *consecutively*. We might shorten the process of taking in the information if we learn to speed-read, but it is still a serial process, whereas taking in a visual image is a parallel one. What then is the remedy?

According to Eugene Vale, in his book *The Technique of Screenplay Writing*, the solution is as old as Homer. While there is an unavoidable inconsistency between the consecutive intake of successive words and the concurrent intake of visual imagery, there is no such clash if the words are strung together *to describe action*.

Action? You may ask. But aren't we talking about *description*?

Yes indeed we are, but the narrative voice, used to report action, may also be used to convey descriptive imagery *indirectly*. The description may be smuggled in with a few adjectives or conveyed in a narrative passage its own right. Vale gives the Homeric example of a warrior preparing for battle by putting on his helmet and then picking up his shield and finally grasping his sword. Instead of merely describing the warrior with these accoutrements of battle, Homer describes the process of preparation as a narrative so that by the end of the narrative the reader will see, in his mind's eye, the warrior replete with his helmet, shield and sword. The point is that at no stage are we asked to stop and *look* at the warrior. Rather, the warrior is *doing* something at all times, but as a result of *what* he does, we see him as a completed image, without dwelling on how he got there.

There are plenty of examples of using the narrative voice to convey description in contemporary thrillers too.

And it does not even have to be such an elaborate process as the warrior "girding his loins" for battle. It can just as easily be a simple event with a couple of adjectives thrown in. Here is an example of the process in its simplest form from Denise Danks's *Frame Grabber*.

> Richard Monroe jabbed a spade-shaped, nail-bitten finger on the dusty computer screen.

And here's another.

> A young black man, trim in his green uniform with shiny brass buttons, entered with our third and final tray of drinks.

What is so good about this approach is its simplicity. The author doesn't hold up the story with a description, even a short one. She simply works the relevant adjectives into the narrative. She doesn't pause the action to tell us what the actors look like, she let's us "see" them *while* they are in action.

Another good example of this elegantly simple approach is given by Thomas Harris in *The Silence of the Lambs*.

> Clarice Starling flinched as the first heavy steel gates crashed shut behind her and the bolt shone home. Chilton walked slightly ahead, down the green institutional corridor in an atmosphere of Lysol and distant slammings.

No static description like "There *were* heavy steel gates" or "the corridor *was* green and institutional.." No need: they are walking down the corridor while the inserted adjectives flesh out the picture and make it three dimensional.

111

This is a good technique to remember precisely because it is relatively simple to apply – as long as you are conscious of what you are doing. Why say "his hair was gray but full" (as I did in an early draft of my first novel) when you can say "he flicked a strand of gray hair out of his eyes" to convey the same meaning?

Not only can one insert a description into a narrative passage by the inclusion of appropriate adjectives, but one can also use *verbs* — more traditionally associated with narration — as *tools of description*. Again, to quote Peter J Ognibene's *The Big Byte*.

> A swarm of fat, wet snowflakes, defined in the yellow-white beams of the van's headlights, suddenly floated up and enveloped the windshield. Steady as a metronome, the wipers beat a path through the advancing snow. Willard squirmed uncomfortably in the high-backed driver's seat.

Note how the snowflakes are "defined" (a verb, not an adjective) in the headlights and how they "floated up" – another verb. Also note how they "enveloped" the windshield and the wipers "beat" a path. There is an important lesson in this; verbs can substitute for adjectives when used appropriately. But that is not to say that adjectives are absent from the passage. On the contrary: the snowflakes are "fat" and "wet" while the beams of the headlamps are "yellow-white". Even the verb "advancing" is used as an adjectival verb when applied to the snow.

But it is the verbs that make this description flow. Without them it would be static and flat. It is the verbs in this description that bring it to life and while Willard may be squirming "uncomfortably", the reader is most comfortable to read such a good description.

Another good example of the use of verbs as descriptive tools can be seen in Ayn Rand's masterpiece *Atlas Shrugged*.

> Things streaked past — a water tank, a tree, a shanty, a grain silo. They had a windshield wiper motion: they were rising, describing a curve and then dropping back. The telegraph

wires ran a race with the train, rising and
falling from poll to pole, in an even rhythm,
like the cardiograph record of a steady
heartbeat written across the sky.

In addition to its use of verbs as building blocks of a description, this passage also illustrates another principle I discussed earlier: describing facts and underscoring them with a summary of their meaning. The significance of the last sentence in the quoted passage is that many people in the story were skeptical about whether the train journey being described was safe to make – especially when it came to crossing a newly-constructed bridge. The character whose point of view is being described, is a woman who runs a railroad and who insisted on building this railroad line – and the bridge – out of a new metal alloy, in the face of strenuous opposition from the skeptics and doubters.

Chapter 6 - What about the narrative voice?

The narrative voice in essence

We have already seen that the descriptive voice conveys sensory data: the look, sound, feel, smell and taste of people, places, food and objects. The narrative voice conveys *action*. This means not only what people do, but also what the forces of nature do. An account of the destructive effect of a hurricane is as much narration as an account of a gunman on the rampage through a shopping mall.

What type of events might be presented in the narrative voice? The list is almost endless: murder, adultery, discovery of a body or a cache of money or drugs, a car crash, a couple planning their honeymoon, a space flight, three friends on a shopping spree.

Of course the narrative relating these events to the reader will almost certainly be punctuated by dialogue and in many cases also by description. But the narrative will be of vital importance in relaying the information to the reader. Even when information is conveyed with dialogue – with one person describing what another person *did* – it is actually the *narrative voice* that is being used. It is just that it is enclosed in quotation marks and coming from one of the characters. For example, if the finding of a body is described not by the third person author directly but by one of the characters telling another, the character giving the information is using the narrative voice.

Thus, just as description can sometimes be an objective message in a subjective envelope, so information can be revealed to the reader as a narrative message in a "dialogue envelope".

Like description, narration can assume many styles and take on many forms. The writer's choice of style depends on such factors as the genre of the story, the writer's viewpoint (first person, third person subjective, etc.) and most importantly the *purpose* for which narration is being used.

The reason I speak of the *purpose* for which narration is being used is because the narrative voice as a tool in the writer's toolbox has many potential purposes and functions. *Advancing the plot* is the most obvious of those functions. However, it may also be used as a means for *establishing the characterization* of the people in the story. Furthermore, when narration takes place in flashback, it can also be used to *explain the background* to the story so that subsequent events become more intelligible. Finally, as we have already seen in the last chapter, the narrative voice can be used to *create a descriptive image* in the reader's mind.

Advancing the plot

The most obvious use of the narrative voice is of course to advance the plot. For this purpose it is *marginally* more important than dialogue and *considerably* more important than description. Characters may say things and what they say is undoubtedly important. By the process of dialogue they reveal information to each other, which motivates them to further action. Changes in their state of knowledge may also have a vital impact on their behavior, and thus on the story itself. But the dialogue in itself is only the *precursor* to their action. It should not be confused with the action itself.

Thus it is the action that moves the story forward!

There are many different types of action that can advance a story. It might be a major event like a murder, a daring rescue, a proposal of marriage or a calamitous mishap. It might be the discovery that ones partner is cheating. It could be the disappearance of a priceless of object. It could be chance meeting. It could even be something that does not appear to have significance yet, but will have repercussions later. Thus the action that drives the story forward can be major or minor.

How might a major event be narrated in a story? There are many ways. It depends on the genre and the viewpoint being used. Here is an example from my first novel *A Fool for a Client* written in the author omniscient viewpoint. The passage is actually *predominantly* third person *objective*, but with a trace of insight into the thought process, first of one character and then of the others who are acting in concert with one another.

In the extract, a member of the Irish splinter group INLA is being tortured by members of the IRA to find out about their plans. The viewpoint is that of the victim.

> His head was shaking frantically from side to side and the tears were streaming down his face in anticipation of the searing agony. The drill advanced towards his left knee-cap. He tried to free his leg but it was secured firmly by the ropes. The drill made contact with his knee, cutting firmly into the bone and sending a spasm of unbearable agony up his body to his brain.

> Even through the gag he emitted a heart-rending cry of pain. But to his interrogators, heart-rending was a concept devoid of meaning. The smaller IRA man pulled off the tape. Padraig spat out the sock and coughed as he gasped for air. He was choking on his tears of torment, knowing that he may well have suffered permanent damage already, and knowing that after this he would have to go into hiding lest the INLA kill him in the most painful fashion for the act of treachery he was about to commit.

First of all you are hit by the fact that the imagery is quite graphic. The narrative does not pull its punches in its explicit description of the process of torture. It would of course be possible to make the narrative even more graphic — and gory — but it is pretty intense even as is. This is not to shock the reader, but rather to create a state of mind commensurate with the significance of what is being narrated within the context of the story as a whole. The events in the quoted passage are clearly a major watershed in the story. Some one is being tortured and is about to give out information that he would rather conceal. This in turn will enable others to set off on a major course of action and the graphic nature of the description befits the significance of the event in the story.

Another feature is that in addition to being graphic, there is an element of *cinematographic* traditionalism about it. We cut between a CLOSE SHOT of the victims head ("his head was shaking frantically from side to side and the tears were streaming down his face"), a REVERSE ANGLE or POINT-OF-VIEW SHOT of the weapon that threatens so much pain and damage ("the drill advanced towards his left knee-cap") and then a CLOSE-SHOT of his leg as he struggles vainly to get free ("he tried to free his leg but it was secured firmly by the ropes"). Finally, at the risk of our "movie" getting a more adult classification, we get a CLOSE-UP of the damage being done.

The "scene" continues in the next paragraph with a facial CLOSE-UP of Padraig's immediate reaction to the torture, the terrorists' reaction to *his* reaction and only then does it depart from its predominantly objective cinematographic approach and probe Padraig's mind, giving the reader a tentative insight into is going to happen next as the character himself speculates on the future.

Here's another example of the narrative voice in action, this one from John Grisham's *The Chamber,* a book about a man on Death Row and attempts by a lawyer to save him. The passage describes the event that put the man on the road to the death penalty.

> The blast shot upward and horizontally at several thousand feet per second. Fifteen sticks of dynamite in the centre of a wooden framed building will reduce it to splinters and rubble in a matter of seconds. It took a full minute for the jagged slivers of wood and other debris to return to earth. The ground seemed to shake like a small earthquake, and, as witnesses would later describe, bits of glass sprinkled downtown Greenville for what seemed like eternity.

Here again we see a very intense and powerful account of a major event in the story — indeed one of *the* two major events in the story. In the paragraph immediately following this, Grisham too gives a graphic account of the effect of the bombing, on a lawyer and his twin children, continuing the development of the plot.

There is a salutary lesson to be learned from this passage about the scope and limitations of strict rules in the process of creative writing. Some of the so-called "style-checker" computer programs advise writers against using words such as "seemed" — claiming that they are weak and that they detract from the power of a passage. Yet Grisham uses the word "seemed" twice *in one sentence* without detracting in any way from the power of the passage.

This should serve as an important warning not to rely too heavily — if at all — on artificial formulae for writing. Of course the choice of individual words *is* important and certain words are weak as a general rule. But there are no hard and fast rules and if one is describing the psychological impact of an event upon *people*, what better way to convey the emotions and sensory perceptions of the people than to say "it seemed"?

And here's another example from my thriller *15 Hours*.

> Then it happened.
>
> Alex was at the curve that overlooked Gull Rock. He had to make a sharp right turn to take him away from the cliff face and then a hairpin turn to the left to take him back to the cliff face, which was shallower from then on.
>
> But he never even made it to the hairpin turn. It may have been the tires. It may have been oil on the road. But when he made the sharp right turn he lost control of the car and it skidded off the road and onto a steep decline. At this point, the cliff was bare of foliage that might offer traction or friction.
>
> Nat screamed, while Alex struggled frantically to regain control as he saw the car heading for that sheer drop onto the rocks below. Somehow he managed to hold it together for a split second, so they missed the sheer drop.
>
> They skidded sideways onto a slightly shallower drop where some foliage offered a trace of resistance, but then the car bounced and started tumbling sideways down into a

> steep gully, bouncing every time the roof or
> wheels hit the foliage beneath them.
>
> Their seat belts held them in place but, even
> before they hit the bottom, Alex could see
> blood oozing from Nat's head from the
> impacts.
>
> And then – completely inverted – they hit
> rock bottom amid a shattering of glass. The
> rocks and the ocean waves lapping away at
> them and water flooding into the vehicle.

Of course narrative writing does not have to be all high-intensity action – even when it involves driving a car! A quiet passage *leading up to action* or following action is also narrative, as this passage from the climax of my second book *The Other Victim* shows.

> Michael Digby kept his eyes on the road as
> he drove a long a back road, occasionally
> glancing into the rear-view mirror for signs
> of activity from the back seat. He knew that
> he had nothing to worry about. The injection
> was enough to keep an average-sized adult
> unconscious for at least two hours. But this
> was not something he had done before and
> apprehension was inevitable. He had kept
> him alive as a kind of insurance. If he was
> stopped and found with the boy asleep in the
> back seat of the car he could say he had just
> just fallen asleep or lost consciousness and
> he was rushing him to hospital.

Parenthetically, the first thing the reader may notice is my inept, indeed erroneous, use of the word "apprehension". The reason that this use of the word is so clumsy is that it is ambiguous. Does it mean apprehension as in "fear" or apprehension as in "capture by the authorities"? In fact I meant the former, but the subsequent two sentences, suggest the latter: ("If he was stopped and found…").

It would have been better if I had said "apprehensiveness" (an abstract noun formed from the adjective apprehensive) or alternatively used the phrase "his sense of apprehension" which would have cleverly retained the ambiguity and yet been equally applicable in both its meanings.

A purist or critical reader may also notice the ambiguous — almost Biblical — use of the pronouns "he" and "him". On at least two occasions the reader is forced to resort to pragmatic analysis (i.e. looking at the context) to avoid semantic ambiguity (i.e. confusion over the literal meaning of the pronouns). Who is "he" and who is "him"? In fact, in both cases "he" is Michael Digby and "him" is the unconscious boy. In general it is better be careful with pronouns, avoiding these clumsy ambiguities.

But putting aside this repentant breast-beating, there is much that is good, or at least illuminating — in a positive sense — in this passage. We see how the narrative can move smoothly from an account of some ones actions to an insight into his thoughts about what has happened already and about what might happen.

Describing a person's thoughts in any passage of significant length has been dubbed "stream-of-consciousness." That term, originated by William James in the context of psychology (albeit borrowed from early Buddhist scriptures was later applied to the writings of Dorothy Richardson by the writer and critic May Sinclair. Defined as a "narrative technique whereby the thoughts of one or more characters are recorded," it was popularized – if one can call it that – by James Joyce.

But the operative words there are "narrative technique." Stream-of-consciousness is not some separate art form, or even a separate voice from the narrative voice. It is a sub-category of the narrative voice.

Very often, in writing, the author routinely moves into and out of the thoughts of a character. Even where the passage is in the third-person subjective viewpoint, it need not dwell solely on the characters thoughts. In other words, stream-of-consciousness is almost always either first person or third-person subjective, but not all first person or third-person subjective is stream-of-consciousness.

Of course a characters thoughts can also advance the plot indirectly by clarifying something that has come before that the reader has not yet been told about. And those same thoughts can show how a character is motivated. The following example is from my fourth book *Reckless Justice*.

> In the course of these inquiries, he
> discovered that Grainger was a widower with
> three young children. The man's wife had
> died in a car crash just a few years before.
> And then he started to think about Ruth's
> words…

The passage continues with recollection of their dialogue and then summarizes the critical result of these events: "So he decided to not to execute Grainger… at least not yet." As you can see, a narrative passage doesn't have to be flowery or fancy. A few simple words, saying something in a straightforward way is stylistically just as good as the most fancy phraseology. Sometimes it's better.

In a mystery story, the narrative voice can also be used for the planting of clues. Supposing for example we wish to use the old proverbial "killer was left handed" routine. We can have the detective note, in his thoughts, that the angle of the bullet, entering from the right front of the head suggests that the killer was left-handed. Alternatively we can simply have the pathologist describe the injuries in such a way as to make it clear that they were most likely inflicted by a left-handed person (e.g. a knife wound entering from the victim's right towards the median line).

Then, elsewhere in the narrative we can drop a more subtle clue that the person who is later revealed to be the killer is also left-handed. But what might that clue be?

If it were a British thriller, we might make a brief reference to him holding the fork in his right hand while he eats. But one must be careful of a minor pitfall here, because in the United States, it is quite normal to cut up one's food first and then transfer the fork to ones right hand to eat it. This, apparently, goes back to the days when poor households had only one knife and the father would cut up the food and then hand the knife to his wife who would cut up hers after which the knife would be transferred round the table to the children in order of age

Alternatively, one could have a scene in which the character who turns out to be the killer is using his computer and manipulating the computer's "mouse" with his left hand. But this might seem to obvious, especially if we have already stated explicitly that the killer is left-handed. If we haven't yet stated this then we might get away with it.

But we could make it more subtle still. We could have the killer installing an operating system in his new computer and have him selecting an option to "reverse mouse buttons". Those familiar with personal computers (as people increasingly are) will understand that this means that the buttons are being re-programd so that the left button does what the right button normally does and vice versa. The full significance may not register with their consciousness at the time, but it means that the clue has been provided so that when the denouement comes, they will not feel cheated.

A clue can also be cleverly combined with a red herring. For example, in one of my books, a man was convicted on the strength of evidence that may have been tampered with. At another stage in the book, I described X having certain skills that would have enabled him to do the tampering. A moderately astute reader might well have inferred that X was guilty. But at another point in the story I described how X had given samples of his former work *to his new employer* to show what he could do. Thus the new employer would be able to acquire the same skills, just by looking at the samples of previous work from his new employee. And if X showed these samples to his new employer at the time when he was *seeking* a job, he might also have shown them to *other prospective employers*!

A common ploy in whodunit's is to have the killing done in an unusual way and to have the killer being the only person who has that rare skill. The trick is not to make clear the full mechanics of how the killing was done, but to present enough information about it to make it part of the mystery ("the killer must have fled on foot, but there were no footprints in the wet sand"). Then elsewhere, you slip in a clue as to the rare skill of the person who is to be revealed as the killer. ("He was polishing the trophy he had won ten years ago in the paragliding contest.")

In practice a good writer will usually use a combination of narrative and dialogue to convey this information.

Use of the narrative voice to assist in characterization

As we saw in the above example, the narrative voice can also play a major part in developing characters and conveying information about them to the reader. Here is another example, this time from an thriller of mine originally called *No Way Out*, published by HarperCollins UK (Avon UK imprint).

> He tried to soften the pain by reminding himself of what had driven him to do the things he had done and become the man he became. But those memories were even *more* painful. Like the time he was nine when two white policemen raped his mother before his eyes. He had tried to stop them, but one of them had grabbed him and twisted his arm behind his back, forcing him to watch while the other "pig" had pinned his mother to the ground, ripped her clothes and forced himself into her as she screamed and begged for mercy.

In this passage, the character is remembering some of the events of his childhood that led to him going on to become a member of a militant organization in his twenties. This in turn is relevant to the character now, when he is in his sixties, because his past has come back to haunt him in the story.

The narrative above is a fairly straightforward account of past events that shaped a character's personality. But conveying information about a characters thoughts and mental state does not have to be so direct. There are in fact some very ingenious narrative devices for conveying a characters state of mind, but not all of them are suitable for the written medium.

For example, there is a famous scene in the film *I Want to Live* in which a lawyer whose client has been sentenced to death shuts off his hearing aid to cut off the outside world with which he has become disillusioned. This is accompanied by a cutting out of the sound from the film so that the viewer shares the experience from the lawyer's point of view.

123

Now obviously this wouldn't work in a book. But one can always find variations on the theme. One example of this is to be found in John Grisham's *The Chamber*. In that story, a lawyer who has been fighting for the client on Death Row, goes out to buy some cans of beer. When told that he cannot buy beer after midnight he asks the sales assistant "Do you know what I think of the laws of this state right now?" So far, the information has been conveyed with dialogue. But then – after the woman in the shop has told him that she doesn't care what he thinks – the author continues with narrative:

> Adam flipped a ten-dollar bill on the counter
> and carried the beer back to his car. She
> watched him leave, then stuck the cash in her
> pocket and went back to the phone. Why
> bother the cops over a six-pack of beer?

At one level this is a very simple statement of the hero's actions and another person's reaction to them. But at another level it is a very powerful way of conveying the disillusion that the character — a lawyer — feels about the law. Simple words, used in a complex way: very effective.

Using the narrative voice to delve into a character's thoughts does not have to be direct or straightforward. The writer can also use interesting metaphors or analogies. Here's an example from my psychological thriller *Tarnished Heroes*. It narrates a scene from the start of the book in which a woman with a mysterious past is walking alone at night, while sensing that she is being followed by a man who had immediately prior to that been watching surreptitiously in a nearby bar:

> She had almost reached the end where the
> road and footpath drew level with one
> another. Ahead of her, to the left just across
> the road, she saw the Old Bull and Bush, the
> public house immortalized in a celebrated
> music hall sing-along. The Old Bull and
> Bush, or North End, the street that ran by it,
> were the alternative names of an old
> underground station on the Northern Line
> between Hampstead and Golders Green that

had been excavated at platform level in 1907
but never opened. The thought of an unused
hole in the ground made her wince. It was
like a grave, waiting for some one to be
buried. But then again, she realized, maybe it
was just her fears that needed to be laid to
rest — the fears that had haunted her since
the day she had looked at the pictures of a
helpless young woman who lay blood-
soaked and dead on Hampstead Heath.

Here the story blends immediate experience with memory and
Freudian metaphor. We have the message delivered by the narrative
voice alone, unaided by the handmaid of dialogue.

However, as the example from Grisham's *The Chamber* illustrated,
combining dialogue with narration can be a very effective way of
illuminating a character's mindset. In Edward Stewart's brilliant
political thriller *They've Shot the President's Daughter*, a young man
who works for a public relations firm has just explained in detail to
the head of a government security agency why he wrote an elaborate
response to a simple internal memo asking the staff how one might
create, respectively, the most and the least sympathy for the
president. After the character has gone through his single-spaced,
nine-page response, the head of the agency asks him why.

'Once I got started, it was hard to stop. One
thing dovetailed into another.'

Woodrow Judd eyed the apple-cheeked boy
amiably, as though they shared a secret.
'And maybe you were bucking for
promotion?'

Jordie's became the smile of an angel caught
out.

The passage contains dialogue, description and narrative combined.
But it is Jordie's reaction – the smile – that underlines his state of
mind. It is basically a narrative description in response to dialogue.

It is rare to find a passage of narrative that conveys information
about a character's state-of-mind unaided by dialogue. But that then
again narrative is almost always interspersed with dialogue and

125

description, whatever its purpose as we saw with in the case of the writer planting clues,. That is not to say that long blocks of uninterrupted narrative *never* occur. But such long uninterrupted narrative passages are usually found in the most climactic phases of the story, when the plot has to advance rapidly or in a major way. Such climactic phases of the story typically include chase scenes, pursuit scenes and fights between hero and villain.

Most narrative, however, is intermingled with dialogue and it is usually more comfortable to the reader to have it so mingled. For this reason alone it makes sense to use the combination of narrative and dialogue to achieve whatever one is trying to achieve. Nevertheless, it must be reiterated that people are characterized more by what they *do* than by what they *say*. What people *say* expresses what they *aspire* to be; what they *do* expresses what they *are*. Thus narrative can be used not only to show the events that shaped a person and made them what they became (as in the example from *Binary Justice* above) but also to show them as they are now.

With this in mind, here is a passage that shows the true nature of a mild-mannered woman Detective Chief Inspector, Karen Rousson when she encounters a case of road rage. The background to the incident is that her car is stuck behind another car that has a stalled engine. There is nothing she can do about this. But Karen doesn't get angry with the driver in front of her. She understands that he is an inexperienced driver and that he isn't doing in on purpose.

But the driver behind her, on the other hand, is a low-brow "macho" type who keeps honking his horn aggressively, as if this is going to solve the problem. In response to this behavior, Karen gets out and tries to reason with him, explaining that the driver of the car in front isn't doing it deliberately. But the road rage driver doesn't care. All that matters to him is that he is facing inconvenience and like a two-year-old, he throws a tantrum.

> She turned and walked slowly back to her car, listening with amusement as he cursed and swore at her. Then she closed the door, but made sure not to lock it. She opened the glove compartment, looked in the rear-view

mirror and waited. It took only a few seconds for the irate driver to open his door and come storming out. She moved her hand from the glove compartment to her lap, her index finger tensing slightly. When he reached the door, he didn't hesitate.

"Why the fuck aren't you moving, you stupid fuckin' bitch?

Again she smiled sweetly, showing not the slightest trace of fear, although she felt some. She knew that he was probably reluctant to use violence here. He would settle for intimidation. But she knew that her apparent lack of fear angered him all the more. It meant that his wishes were frustrated. And frustrated intentions were what road rage was all about; that and lack of control.

"Well, I can't move now because my door's open," she said, showing white teeth and an amused contempt for his frustration.

With the ferocity of an animal that had just been attacked, he reached in and grabbed her by the right lapel of her jacket, trying to yank her out of the car so that he could take a more powerful swing at her with greater freedom of movement. But without resisting his pulling motion, she brought her left hand up and sprayed him in the face with pepper spray.

Unlike the passage from *No way Out* which narrated an event from the past which showed how the character was shaped into what he became, this passage merely describes a revealing incident that tells us what sort of a person DCI Karen Rousson really is. It shows us what a tough cookie she is, but it doesn't tell us how she got that way. This does not make the earlier passage "better", it merely means that each passage is doing what the author set out to do. It is up to you as the author to decide how much you want to reveal of your characters and when. If you are writing a psychological thriller, you might want to stagger the revelations, or reveal them in stages, showing first what they are and *then* how they became that way.

Explaining the background through narrative

As we saw with the example from *No Way Out* about the man remembering his mother being raped, when he was a boy, the narrative voice can be used to fill in the background, referring to past events that render the story intelligible. In the example above, the narrative voice was used to offer insight into how a man's character was shaped by a traumatic experience. But the narrative voice can be used more generally to relate past events that are relevant to the story in a whole variety of ways.

Supposing for example two of the major characters are an Israeli intelligence officer and a young Irish woman who came to Israel as a Catholic pilgrim and – after a traumatic incident – went on to become an Israeli and also an officer in the Israeli Mossad. How we might start narrating the background.

> Sarit and Dov went back together some four years, when she was the eager young twenty-year-old immigrant from Ireland, fresh out of her two-year army service. In those days, she was called Siobhan Stewart. At eighteen, she had left her sheltered middle-class life in Cork and volunteered to work in Israel and ended up staying. The trigger for her decision had been a visit to the Holy Land the previous year with her family during which her brother had been killed in a suicide bombing in Jerusalem by Arab terrorists, along with twenty-one other people. She herself had been one of the 135 wounded, albeit comparatively mildly.

> After that she had tried to understand both sides in the conflict and not merely jump to a conclusion based on emotions alone. But what she found particularly galling were the one-sided condemnations when Israel retaliated against the organizers and planners

of a whole spate of similar suicide bombings that followed.

So the following year, bypassing the more traditional picking-apples-on-a-kibbutz option, she had volunteered for eight weeks of equally menial duty on an Israeli army base under the auspices of an organization called Sar-El. It was soon discovered that she had a sharp mind and was a fast learner and so she ended up being given duties that a foreign volunteer would not normally be trusted with.

This was followed by her bold decision to apply for permanent residence and volunteer for a full two years of service in the Israeli army, much to the horror of her parents. After some gruelling interviews to test her sincerity, and in the face of plaintive appeals to come home, she was accepted by the Israeli army and spent the next two years serving in communications. She also changed her name in that time to the more Israeli-sounding Sarit Shalev.

This passage is from my thriller *The Moses Legacy*. Obviously there is a lot more background. But it would be wrong to continue with it at this time. Background passages should be broken up into fragments and interspersed with the rest of the story. Otherwise, we low down the narrative or even bring it to a grinding halt.

Writing description in the narrative voice

We have seen in the previous chapter how the narrative voice can be used to convey descriptive information. Here's an example of the technique applied to a place. The passage is taken from my first book *A Fool for a Client*. In the passage, the heroine is following a man whom she intends to kill. But she is not ready to kill him just yet. At this stage she is merely following him to learn about him, to establish his routine and find out what sort of places he likes to go to, in preparation for what she intends to later.

As the sun sank like a smoldering flame and the city dissolved into the bland, lifeless tone of the evening twilight, she had followed him like a panther stalking its quarry. She had followed him past greasy pimps and heavily painted hookers. She had followed him past the stooges of the sidewalk con artists as they enticed the mark into a rigged three-card monte. She had watched him from the shadows of the ethnic ghettos as he strolled and played the game of living footloose in New York. She had tailed him through the singles bars and pick-up joints. She knew him inside out. She had seen him change the color of his personality like a grass snake as he slithered through the slums and sewers of the concrete jungle.

Occasionally she glanced up at the penthouses above for a moment's relief from the cockroaches and sewer rats below...

As the curtain of dusk descended around her, she looked up at the majestic towers of the skyline, drawing comfort from the squares of light hanging there in the night sky like sparkling gems against black velvet. These were the windows of the penthouses, where the curtains never needed to be drawn against the darkness, where the sense of adventure was untainted by the stench of the garbage that littered the streets.

She kept to the shade, avoiding the misty pools of light thrown by the tall, lean street lamps onto the cold gray stone of the sidewalk. From lightless corners she had observed him like a zoologist observes his laboratory specimens. She had studied him in action while he spotted his prey and homed in for the kill. She knew every movement and physical gesture of his routine. The only thing she didn't know where the words. But these didn't matter. She would find out soon enough. The important thing was that she knew what kind

of girl he liked. She knew the look… and she
knew the type.

As you can see in this passage we have a predominantly narrative
voice but the voice is used to advance the story *and* to build up a
visual picture. The picture is built up partly by the insertion of
adjectives alongside the nouns that they qualify: "*greasy* pimps",
"*heavily painted* hookers", "*bland, lifeless* tone", "*majestic* towers",
"*sparkling* gems", "*misty* pools of light", "*cold grey* stone",
"*lightless* corners"). But we also have the narrative voice, replete
with its characteristic verbs, to flesh out the picture: "the sun *sank*",
"the city *dissolved*", "she had *followed* him," "*stalking* its quarry",
"*watched* him", "She had *seen* him", "he *slithered*", "she *glanced*
up", "She *kept to* the shade.", "he *spotted* his prey", and "he *homed*
in for the kill".

While only some of these verbs contribute directly to the description
itself, they all serve to keep the passage squarely in the narrative
voice, maintaining a constant stream of action while the visual image
is planted in the reader's mind. At no stage is the reader likely to
stop and think: "I'm reading a description." Rather there is a feeling
of important events taking place even as the picture is assembled.

The above is, as I pointed out, a description of a place
(predominantly) created using narrative tools. But it is also possible
to use the narrative voice to convey a description of a person. Later
in that same chapter we read about Justine, the heroine, getting
dressed in her sexiest clothes as she prepares for her first meeting
with the man she intends to kill.

> She went over to the full-length mirror, still
> wearing the bathrobe, Even modestly
> covered up, with only the calves and
> forearms to hint at the shape of the rest, there
> was no denying the beauty that would carry
> the plan through to midfield…
>
> She sat down on the bed, slipped her arms
> out of the bathrobe and threw it behind her.
> There was a brusque anger in her movements
> as she picked up the tight-fitting purple T-
> shirt, pulled it over her head and smoothed it

down over her body. It was followed by a
pair of frilly briefs of black lace…

The purple shorts came next. They matched
the T-shirt in both color and style… and
carried the same suggestion. She stepped
into them and pulled them up with s swift
movement. They hugged her form, showing
it at its best…

The combination was complemented by a
pair of high leather boots in white.

It is important remember that ninety nine times out of a hundred a
story is about *movement*, or at least should be. Therefore, description
— whether it is done in the descriptive voice or the narrative voice
— should be used sparingly. Description is to give the reader a sense
of presence at the scene but it is the action that makes it *worthwhile*
for the reader to be present. The advantage of the narrative voice is
that it gives pace to the description and can even be used in a hybrid
form, carrying the action forward and bringing it visually to life at
the same time.

Narrative styles

Although I have spoken of the "narrative voice" in the singular, there
are of course many narrative styles. Let's take another passage from
Edward Stewart's political thriller *They've Shot the President's
Daughter*.

At 12:12 p.m. a man in hunting boots and
blue jeans and a checked sports shirt entered
the First Methodist Church of Whitefalls. He
had the sort of windburned face that inspires
trust and sells cigarettes. He was stopped
inside the door by a Secret Service man who
asked his business. He said he wanted to
pray.

The Secret Service man apologized that the
church was not open to the public till after
the ceremonies in the graveyard. The bell
tower, he explained, offered far too inviting
a perch for snipers. The man smiled and said

he understood. 'The times we live in,' were his words.

He turned as though to go, and the Secret Service man made the mistake of glancing away. Something struck him in the back of the neck and that was all he remembered before he crumpled.

The man in blue jeans, who had learned the blow in counter-insurgency school, withdrew a disposable, preloaded syringe from the breast pocket of his checked sports shirt.

Note how in this passage the dialogue is narrated rather than quoted. This has the effect of playing down its *form*, but not its *content*. The precise words are not all that important, and even when they are quoted directly it is by way of ironic comment on the theme of the book as a whole.

The overall effect of the passage, in the book, is to build up the tension. It prepares us for something big. We are told about a "perch" being tempting to "snipers", so we know where the story is going — even without reference to the title.

Narrative can be tough and gritty, flowing and contemplative, bitter and ironic. Both the genre of the book and the writer's individual temperament will have an influence on the style. Let's compare some examples. First a passage from a writer of what might be called modern classic thrillers. The book is *Innocent Blood* and the author is the legendary P. D. James.

The letter was more difficult to write than even the most challenging of her weekly school essays. It was astonishing that a short passage of English prose should take so long to compose, that even the most ordinary words should carry such a charge of innuendo, condescension or crass insensitivity.

The letter in question is being written by a girl who was adopted to her birth mother who has exercised her rights under the Children Act of 1975 to find out who her biological parents were. She has

133

discovered that her mother was a murderess who murdered a child and who is due to be released on license. As she agonizes over the wording of the wording of the letter, the mental tension slowly mounts. The style of the passage shows the intelligence of the girl, written as it is from the third-person subjective viewpoint. This is important because whenever a passage is written from a character's point of view (whether in the first person or third-person subjective) the style (as well as the content) should reflect that character.

Now contrast the style with the following from an American police detective story called *End Game* by Dev Stryker.

> As Joe straightened up, an abrupt punch in the stomach made him gasp and double over. Hiram pulled a weighted sap from his jacket pocket and hit him several times in the face, then began kicking him when Joe fell to the ground.
>
> Joe lay in the fetal position, trying to cover himself up from injury, and Hiram straddled him from behind, looped one arm around his throat and lifted him to his feet.
>
> Then Joe saw the glint of a knife in front of him. He saw it, then felt it plunge into his stomach. Joe groaned and tried feebly to ward off the knife, waving his arms in front of him.

There are yet more extreme examples of the difference between a quiet contemplative style and a tough gritty one. But this comparison is more than enough to illustrate the point.

Now I am not saying that P. D. James is incapable of writing a passage with violence — although she prefers to hint at it with subtle, skillful suggestion (the before and after approach) rather than to spell it out in graphic and gory detail. Nor am I saying that the writing partnership that is Dev Stryker are incapable of writing a subtle, contemplative passage. All I am saying is that there are different styles to suit different authors and different genres.

Chapter 7 – How do I write crackling dialogue?

What is Dialogue?

Dialogue, in essence is quoted speech between two or more persons. Technically, dialogue between two people is called duologue.

In practice three-way and four way conversations are far less common in literature than the proverbial two-way conversation. Just as in Shakespearean drama the monologue was a powerful device for giving the viewer insight into a major character's thoughts, so in literature, dialogue is the staple diet that propels the plot significantly.

Dialogue can be used to advance the plot in a number of ways. The most obvious way is exposition – to give information to the reader. Another is to use it as a device to cause information to be conveyed by one character to another so that the recipient of the information will act on the information in some way. Dialogue can also be used as a tool of characterization: showing what people *are* by what they *say*. Of course what they *do* is even more important. But what they say is part of their character and dialogue is therefore an important tool of characterization, along with narrative and descriptive writing.

Dialogue as a tool of characterization

Dialogue can be used as a tool to convey the nature, thoughts or background of a character in a variety of ways. First and foremost it shows the state of mind of the speaker. Secondly the content of the speech can carry information about others. Thirdly the interaction of the speech by the parties conveys information about the relationship between them.

These elements are not discrete elements that can be isolated one from another. They can be present in combinations, overlapping with one another. Here's an excellent example from Edward Stewart's *They've Shot the President's Daughter*.

> "Bill. Listen to me and understand me. Lexie and I are leaving you."
>
> "You're not making sense."
>
> "I'm taking Lexie to my father's for a long, long time. I want to get her away from this place. You can tell the press that she's recuperating and that I'm recuperating too. I won't be with you any more Bill. And I won't leave Lexie here with you."
>
> "You talk as though I posed some kind of danger to my own daughter."
>
> "You're the president. Wherever you go, there'll be bullets and reporters."
>
> He gripped her shoulder. "For God's sake Moni, I love you."
>
> She dried her eyes with the back of her hand. "What about your daughter? Do you love her?"
>
> "What the hell is wrong with you? Of course I love her."
>
> "Then let her go Bill. And let me go with her."
>
> The First Lady rose from the chair. The President reached a hand but did not stop her. There was concern and there was bafflement in the tilt of his head. "I've never seen you this way before."
>
> "You've never looked at me."

The dialogue here tells you about the state of mind of each speaker. But it also tells you about the relationship and about the other. In this case there is only limited information about the third party, their daughter Lexie. But we know that she exists and that she is in some sort of danger.

137

Now, let's take a simple made-up example. To set the scene: a man has just walked through the front door into his house. His coat is still on when his wife speaks.

> "Your dinner's cold."
>
> "I was doing my job."
>
> "You're always doing your job. Even when you're here at the weekend, you're doing your job."
>
> "The company needs me."
>
> "And *I* don't?"
>
> "If I don't pull my weight now, I could find myself out on the street."
>
> "Is that what it's all about? You think Charlie's after your job?"
>
> "Charlie's been after my job for the last three years. The only thing that's changed is that now he's in a position to get it."

Even without adverbial phrases, we can "hear" how the lines are being spoken. The background is obvious: a wife who feels that her husband is neglecting her by devoting so much effort to his job; a man fighting to hold onto his job out of fear of a backstabbing colleague. Just from the dialogue, we learn something about three people the husband, the wife and the colleague Charlie. The opening exchange immediately shows what's on their respective minds:

> "Your dinner's cold."
>
> "I was doing my job."

The fact that he answers what she appears to be *thinking*, rather than the actual words that she spoke, tells us a lot. It shows that the problems in their relationship have been developing for some time now, that they've probably had similar discussions before. It tells us that in spite of the strain on their relationship, they do *understand* each other, even if they are struggling to find common ground.

138

This example illustrates something called *sub-text*: the secondary meaning beneath the words. This powerful tool is one of the devices that can separate ordinary dialogue from interesting dialogue. Of course, not all speech has to have sub-text. And there are other ways of making dialogue interesting as we shall see. But the writer should be aware of the possibilities of sub-text and be ready and think about it when appropriate. It is very often the skillful use of sub-text that marks the difference between ordinary dialogue and good dialogue.

A character's vocabulary and style of speech can also indicate their personality and their socio-economic background. Let's take a look at series of statements in both British and American English:

> "I reported him to the police."
>
> "I told the cops about him."
>
> "I informed on him."
>
> "I grassed him up."
>
> "I betrayed him."
>
> "I snitched on him."
>
> "I was a grass."
>
> "I turned stoolie."
>
> "I sang like a canary."

They all suggest a similar act, but the different wording implies differences as to the social class and nationality of the speakers, as well as their prior relationship with the third party.

For example, the first statement — "I reported him to the police" suggests some one British who is middle to upper class. But it could either be a worker betraying a colleague to whom he may have some ambivalent feelings of duty or loyalty, or a person making a criminal complaint about some one who had wronged him, a noisy neighbor or a dangerous driver, for instance. The second is less social-class-specific, but more American.

The statement, "I informed on him," is British, but very distinctly suggests a worker reporting a crime (or breach of some rules or code of conduct), possibly that of a fellow worker. One doesn't "inform" on some one who has robbed one, but one might "inform" on a dishonest colleague, or a fellow doctor who has been drinking while on duty or perhaps a member of a religious order who has been sneaking into strip shows!

When we move from "I informed on him" to "I grassed him up," we are back to British working class – possibly even from *within* the criminal community. The speaker is not *necessarily* a fellow criminal of the party he "grassed up", but he certainly *could* be. However, he (or she) clearly belongs to the lower end of certain socio-economic spectrum.

"I betrayed him," has yet another set of connotations. It tells us nothing about the social class of the speaker, or even the gender. It could be a woman speaking about her husband or boyfriend, or a mother who betrayed her son. But it doesn't have to be. What it *does* tell us is that the speaker felt that they *owed some loyalty* towards the other party. They may feel that they did the right thing (legally or morally) to "betray" them, but this is tinged by the nagging doubt because of the pre-existing sense of duty or loyalty.

"I snitched on him," is in some ways the American equivalent of "I grassed him up," although it could be used by a British character too. Similarly, "I *was* a grass," is clearly a lower class Briton describing his own actions. But the use of the past continuous "was" suggests that he was an informant over a period of time (possibly a *paid* informant), or that he blew the whistle on several people at the same time.

"I turned stoolie," would be the American equivalent, probably implying that the speaker was a criminal associate of those on whom he "snitched". The fact that he "turned" implies that he was one of them and that for some reason (e.g. found God or got caught and cut a deal) he decided to switch sides. Finally "I sang like a canary," also clearly conveys a criminal who testified against his associates — or at least gave the authorities information about them. But this time, it is clear explicitly from the wording that the reason he did it was to save his own skin.

These are of course relatively simple examples of how speech defines the speaker as well as revealing information about the speaker's circumstances. And of course similar circumstances are described differently by the different types of speaker. A working class man who is being arrested for hitting his wife (possibly fatally) might try to weasel out of it by saying: "I just lost me rag and belted 'er. Honest Guv, I didn't mean no 'arm." An upper-middle class man in the same position might try to mitigate the same crime and slither off the hook with words like: "I just lost my self-control for a split-second and lashed out at her without thinking, Inspector. I don't know what came over me."

Of course speech indicates not only the speaker's socio-economic background, it also tells us their *attitude*. Thus, if our working class wife-beater had a more self-centered and morally blind attitude, he might try to rationalize his violence towards his wife by blaming her rather than trying to portray his own action as a momentary lapse. "I kept telling 'er to shut up, but she wouldn't listen," the working-class wife-beater might say. If his upper-middle-class or upper-class counterpart shared this egotistic attitude he would more likely say: "She just kept going on at me, trying my patience until I snapped! Oh don't look at me like that Inspector, you didn't have to *live* with her!"

It is unlikely that either of our two villains will save their miserable skins by taking this arrogant line of defense. Nor will these statements endear the defendants to the judge when their lawyers try to plead in mitigation. But as we read these lines, we see these men for what they are.

One can learn an awful lot about a person from even the briefest of remarks or exchanges. Watch how Peter J Ognibene gives a powerful insight into one of his characters in *The Big Byte*.

> "Look, I never would've gotten involved in this whole damn thing if I'd thought you were going to back out."

> "I am not abrogating out agreement, Willard."

"Don't call me that."

"Sorry. It was a slip of the tongue."

"That's the name my old man gave me. He's
the only asshole that ever called me that.
Except for a couple of asshole teachers."

With a minimum of dialogue, the author tells us that the character called "Willard" has a chip on his shoulder – and hinted strongly at the source of that chip.

In my first thriller, *A Fool for a Client,* I needed to write a scene that would establish the heroine and show how hard she was as a person, but at the same time give a first inkling as to her motives and explain what had made her that way. It was important that I show the heroine as a hard person, because otherwise she would not have the strength of character to do what she does in the story.

But obviously I didn't want to give the whole game away in that passage, early on in the book. My intention was to peel away the layers of her character like an onion throughout the course of the book. However, the scene had to offer the first hint of her character. To do this, I created an interlude between court sessions when she and her court-appointed lawyer have lunch at a local café. The whole chapter is twelve pages. In the following passage, the heroine, Justine, gives a glimpse of her inner self. (Non-dialogue paragraphs have been cut.)

"You're only a stand-by counsel. You don't
have to work at all."

"I could help you on points of law. I could
raise objection to Abrams's tactics and block
evidence that may be harmful to you. But if I
do it blind I could make things worse. Can't
we work together on this one?"

"My defense is going to be very simple: the
truth. I don't need your help with that. I have
nothing to hide and no reason to erect a
barrier of technicalities. Your field is the

law. My concern is the truth. That's what
I'm going to give them."

…

"The way you're carrying on before the jury,
they'll think you're tough enough to commit
murder."

…

"I *am*."

The last part of this tantalizing exchange was used by the publisher
on the back cover of the book. It was important to have such a
dialogue at a relatively early stage of the book, because otherwise
her whole characterization would have fallen apart.

Dialogue can characterize a situation or a cultural ethos or collective
characteristic. Listen to the following dialogue from Ken Follett's
The Eye of the Needle.

> "How are things with you, anyway? You
> don't drop in at the Yard."
>
> "Busy."
>
> "How's Christine?"
>
> "Killed in the bombing."
>
> Harris's eyes widened. "You poor bastard."
>
> "You all right?"
>
> "Lost my brother in North Africa. Did you
> ever meet Johnny?"
>
> "No."
>
> "He was a lad. Drink? You've never seen
> anything like it."

This passage is immensely powerful because of the stark contrast
between the tragic facts that they are discussing and that British stiff-
upper-lip that they display when speaking about it. Note the matter-
of-fact way in which one says "killed in the bombing" when asked
"how's Christine?" No quiet pause, no breaking down in tears: just

a straightforward factual reply. The crisis that caused the death is still going on, and in the face of such hardship they have no time for tears.

Even when the other takes a break from the small talk to express sympathy, it's a tough, brusque type of sympathy: "You poor bastard." No soft soap. But even more than that, the bereaved man does not dwell on his own loss. Instead he asks: "You all right?" When the other one responds with a reference to his own bereavement (to put the two of them on a more equal footing) he goes on to reminisce about a life, not to lament a death.

Perhaps this is because they are men and living in an era when men were not supposed to show sympathy to other men or weakness in themselves. To that extent, it shows an ethos not peculiar to the Second World War or to the British but to the era before the alleged "reconstructed male" or the peace and feminism era of the sixties. Whether the sensitive male who is free to show his feelings is better or worse than his emotionally-repressed counterpart, is a matter for the reader to decide. What the writer does is *characterize* that ethos, bringing it to light through the powerful tool of dialogue – a tool that Follett uses with consummate skill.

Dialogue can also characterize the speaker by showing their intelligence. On a related point, it can also show the speaker's knowledge of facts of the case in particular. This is important, as this sort of display of knowledge is a device not for characterization, but for advancing the plot.

Using dialogue to advance the plot

There are various ways that dialogue can play a role in the advancement of the plot. One way is that it might advance the hero's knowledge, prompting him to act in order to deal with a situation that has arisen. Another is that it can advance the *reader's* knowledge. And of course, these two functions can occur simultaneously, in the same piece of dialogue.

In the following example, from *The Tenth Justice*, by Brad Melzer, a young law graduate, clerking for a Supreme court judge, is trying to contact some one whom he believes to be an ex-clerk for the same judge, who has befriended him and to whom he has talked about the results of cases that have not yet been announced. The old contact number has been disconnected, so he tries the phone company.

"I'm in DC. I'm looking for the phone number of Rick Fagen. F-A-G-E-N." Ben tapped his pen nervously.

"I'm sorry, sir," the operator said. "I have no Fagens listed."

"How about if I give you his old phone number? Can you see if there's a forwarding number?" Ben asked.

"I can try," the operator said. Ben ran to the other side of the room to retrieve the Rolodex card. "Sir, are you there?"

Ben raced back to his desk and sat in his chair. "I'm here." He read off Rick's old number.

"I'm sorry sir," the operator said, "that number is no longer in service."

"I know that," Ben snapped. "That's why I asked if there was a forwarding number." Bristling, he asked, "Can you tell me me where the bill was forwarded to?"

"I'm sorry, we cannot give out that information."

With his panic growing, Ben then tries the accounts payable department, and pretending to be the man that he is looking for he tells them that he didn't get the bill and asks them to check if they have his current address. He draws a blank with this too and then goes on to check the Supreme Court's security records, where he finds out that the man he is looking for in fact never worked there. At that point he realizes that he is in **big trouble**.

The point here is that at each stage, the dialogue makes him aware of the growing problem and thus prompts him to his next action. And because the book is written in such a way that the reader was given no advance warning about what was going on behind the hero's back, this same dialogue is the *reader's* first exposure to these facts. Thus the dialogue serves the duel purpose of informing the reader and prompting the hero to his next action.

Of course this does no always have to be the case. In a story that places the emphasis on suspense, the reader could be notified of these facts ahead of the hero. But Meltzer's book is a mystery as well as a suspense story, and so he surprises us – the readers – along with the hero. Much of the book – though by no means all of it □ is written from the third-person subjective viewpoint, following Ben around and telling us his thoughts. So it make sense for us to be with the hero, and inside his head, when he makes the discoveries that move him forward, and thus for us to make those discoveries at the same time.

Of course, just as dialogue can advance the plot by expanding the hero's knowledge and thus prompting him to action, it can do exactly the same with the *villain*. This can make for very good suspenseful reading. Say, for example, the hero is planning a counter-strike or sting operation against the villain. Then let's say that the villain is told or overhears something that lets him *know* about the hero's plans. At that stage in the story, the *reader* will know that the hero's plans are about to go awry and that the hero may even be in danger. But the hero will now know it. The reader will want to warn the hero or heroine, but will not be able to do so. At that point you will have suspense: that painful emotion that reader's pay good money to experience.

Alternatively, you may spring a surprise on the reader: have the hero *know all along* what is going down and actually be planning something else. In one scenario, the hero might have leaked his purported intentions to the villain all along so that it is the villain who is being lured into a trap. That would make the hero even cleverer and the twist all the more interesting.

146

At the other end of the scale, you could have the hero only discover at the last minute that the plan has gone wrong, forcing him to improvise a quick reserve plan to save himself or whoever else he is trying to save. Or yet you could have the hero walk into the trap and then have to fight or finesse his way out of it.

For now, the most important thing to remember is that dialogue can be used to advance the hero's and the villain's knowledge.

As to the reader's knowledge, it can be updated by the same dialogue as is used to inform the hero (or any character), but doesn't have to be. The reader might be told by the narrative voice that some one was poisoned before the detective is told by the pathologist. We might for example, read how the poisoner prepares the poison or administers it. Then when the hero is told it is no surprise to the reader, but it advances the story as we know that the hero will now proceed to act on the knowledge.

On the other hand, the reader's knowledge might be behind the hero's and the reader might only be informed when the hero tells one of the other characters. This is what happens in the classic whodunit when the detective reveals all to the assembled dramatis personae at the dénouement. But it can happen all the way through and not just at the end. This is very often the case in the "side-kick" model of the detective story. While the story is more likely to be told from the point of view of the sidekick — so as to avoid giving away too much too soon — the flow of information along the way is likely to be towards the side-kick, from the detective. In effect, the side-kick will ask questions and the detective will answer them selectively. Alternatively, the detective will volunteer information, but only in juicy fragments.

One of the most interesting ways in which dialogue is used in thrillers to advance the plot is through the cat-and-mouse game between the hero and the villain. The most common method is to have the villain contacting the hero either directly or indirectly and taunting him.

147

Dev Stryker (an American writing partnership) used this technique to very good effect in a thriller called *End Game* in which a killer is committing murders and leaving the bodies with letters engraved on their heads on various blocks of the New York City street grid. The killer has also left messages for a policeman telling them that the letters stand for pawn, knight and pawn respectively and the police have finally figured out that he is playing a morbid chess game. They have placed an advertisement in the *New York Times* indicating that they are taking up the challenge and now they are waiting for the killer to contact them. The phone rings and the cop who has been receiving the messages, has picked up the receiver.

> "Inspector Regal here," he said.
>
> A shudder went up his neck when he heard the mechanical voice: "For-Inspector-Paul-Regal. I-am-glad-my-challenge-has-been-accepted. White's-next-move-is-bishop-takes-night. As-long-as-the-game-stays-intersting-there-will-be-no-more-killings."
>
> The metallic voice stopped and Regal said, "Hello. Listen to me. Can you hear me? Let's talk about this."
>
> But all he heard back was a click and a dial tone.

This method brings out the suspense as well as the mystery. Dialogue can of course also be used to enable the villain to threaten the hero (or heroine) directly.

But there is, however, another more subtle way of playing out the cat and mouse game. That is when the villain manipulates the hero into acting in a certain way, without revealing himself as the villain. The classic example of this is in Shakespeare's Othello in which Iago manipulates Othello into believing that Desdemona is being unfaithful to him.

In the more modern era, Agatha Christie provided an excellent example of this in the final Hercule Poirot mystery, *Curtain,* written in 1948, but not published until shortly before her death in the 1970s when the motive was a bit anachronistic. In the book, the villain is not known to be the villain until the end (except to clever solutionists like me!) so it is only clear in retrospect what is happening. Nevertheless, the manipulation in the dialogue is an integral part of the story that brings out the "Oh yes! Of course! Why didn't I think of that!" from the reader at the stage of the dénouement.

Dialogue can also advance the by using as a means of laying clues and of describing the discovery of clues. Of course, at the time it may not be clear that it is a clue being discovered.

In the following example from *Dunn's Conundrum* by Stan Lee, an analyst working for an intelligence agency is listening in to a conversation of some people who are viewed by the agency as subversive and whose phone has therefore been tapped.

> "Be patient. I need a little more time," Garvey said.
>
> "There is no more time."
>
> "Who says so?
>
> "The bishop, for one."
>
> "Now I've heard everything. The bishop."
>
> "And the Rabbi."
>
> ...
>
> "The Bishop and the Rabbi," Garvey said. "The experts in political timing."
>
> "Will you listen, Oliver?"
>
> "I'm listening."
>
> "Would you mind telling me what you're waiting for? I've got to have something to tell the others."
>
> "We're waiting for the Doctor. Tell them that."
>
> "How long?"
>
> "Not long."
>
> "Who is the doctor?

"The Doctor is the one who's going to
supply the cure."

"How's he going to do that?" Purefoy said, a
faint, skeptical smile appearing.

"The Doctor's on the inside. On the inside of
the inside, in past the last layer of the onion.
I know what I'm talking about. We'll wait
for the doctor."

Thus begins the search for this mysterious "Doctor" by the agency.
They know that he is not merely working for these conspirators, but
is also *inside* the government camp: a traitor in their midst! What
they *don't* know however is that the conspirators are waiting for him
not in the sense of waiting for his physical arrival or for some action
which he has promised to do for them, but in the sense that he has
yet to see things their way. In effect, they are waiting for him come
round to their point of view! This assumes a great importance when
we discover that the "Doctor" does not know that he *is* the doctor
and is in fact one of the people participating in the surveillance!

In addition to these many uses and applications, as mentioned above,
it is dialogue by which all is revealed at the denouement of a classic
whodunit.

Types of Dialogue

Dialogue can be many things. In relation to characters it can be
hostile, friendly, questioning, romantic. This of course is about the
relationship between the characters. Dialogue can also be crackling,
lethargic, contemplative, unidirectional, rambling. Whichever it is,
it reflects not only the characters as individuals but also the
relationship between them.

One way to make dialogue interesting, according to an article that I
read in a writer's magazine many years ago, is to give the dialogue
what they called a "fire and ice" quality. This means playing on the
inherent inequalities of the characters. Inequalities can itself mean
many things of course. It can be inequality of rank, inequality of
strength or inequality of *knowledge*. The classic example of the last

150

of those, is the experienced wine-waiter who is serving the nouveau-riche customer. Although superficially the customer has the upper hand, by virtue of his wealth, it is actually the "sommelier" (to use the fancy French word) who holds the advantage, because of his knowledge of the different types of wine. He knows which "years" and grape-growing areas produce the best wine and also which types of wine goes with which type of food.

So how might this difference in knowledge work in practice? The most direct way would of course be a straightforward Q & A between the one who wants to know and the one who already knows. The following example is from Jeffrey Archer's *Shall We Tell the President?* Parts of the dialogue, at the start, have been cut for brevity.

> "I need two pieces of information. First, are there any senators with close connections in organized crime and second what is the attitude of the mob to the Gun Control bill?"
>
> "You don't want much, do you?" said the Greek sarcastically. "...when the Mafia needs a senator they do it through a third party, and even that's rare."
>
> "Why?" queried Mark.
>
> "The Mafia needs clout at the state level, in courts, with deals, local by-laws, all that. They're just not interested in foreign treaties and the approval of Supreme Court justices... there are some Senators who owe their success to links with the Mafia, the ones who have started as civil court judges or state assemblymen..."
>
> "Great background. Now can I ask you some specifics. If I name fifteen senators, will you indicate if they could fall into any of the categories you have mentioned?"
>
> "Maybe. Try me. I'll go as far as I feel I can. Just don't push me."
>
> "Bradley."

151

"Never," said Stampouzis.

"Thornton."

He didn't move a muscle.

"Bayh."

"Not that I ever heard."

"Harrison."

"No idea. I don't know much about South Carolina."

"Nunn."

"Sam Sunday-School? Scout's Honor Nunn? You've got to be kidding."

"Brooks."

"Hates the president but I don't think he'd go that far." ...

"Dexter."

He hesitated. Mark tried not to tense.

"Trouble, yes," Stampouzis began. "But Mafia, no."

In this example the process is largely one-way, because of the Q & A nature of the exchange. The fire comes from the man with the answers, the ice from the man asking the questions. But it is also possible to have dialogue based on a more dynamic inequality. The following example is taken from my first thriller *A Fool for a Client*.

"Burning the midnight oil?" asked Jerry, looking over at the desk where Abrams sat.

"Racking my brains over a mystery inside a puzzle."

"The Levy case?" asked the DA, doubtfully.

"The Levy case."

"I thought it was open and shut," said the DA, walking further into the room."

"I'm talking about the why and wherefore. You're talking about *what*, and even that 's not to clear any more."

Jerry sat down on the corner of Abrams's desk.

"What 's the problem?" asked the DA, more out of curiosity than a sympathy."

"A vicious murderer cheats justice because of a judicial ruling that isn't even legally or constitutionally correct. So a girl with no previous record decides to take the law into her own hands. And now she finds herself looking at twenty to life for doing what the courts should've done."

"I never thought I'd live to hear you defending a vigilante."

"I'm not defending her. It's just that I'm not sure I can defend the system either. How can I defend a system either. How can I defend a system that punishes people for fighting back, but lets the hoods slip through the net?"

"You're not defending the system. You're prosecuting a defendant."

"That's *working* the system."

"Correction," the DA shot back hard, "that's *making* the system *work*. It's up to the defense to work the other side of the equation. Besides, you're talking in stale old redneck clichés. That's not like the Daniel Abrams I know, the Daniel Abrams who once said that vigilante justice is a classic example of throwing out the baby with the bathwater."

"That's when I was talking to a middle-class jury. They're not on the front line in the war that's raging out there. They're separated from the combat zone by a thick blue line, manning the trenches. And the same goes for us. We sit behind our mahogany desks and get all the facts in nicely sanitized form. We don't have to look down the barrel of a Saturday-night special like a cop on the street. We just read a report about it afterwards, a load of neatly typed words on clean white paper."

And how does the jury get the facts?" asked Jerry Wilkins. "Words in a courtroom flowing from the lips of a well-rehearsed orator. Juries are drawn from the voting register, the half of the population who choose to participate in the political process, perhaps with a few more thrown in from the driver's license records. They're as sheltered as we are."

"Not this jury," said Abrams. "You should see the collection of down-to-earth hard-heads she put together. Even the businessman on the jury. A self-made millionaire who worked his way up from the gutter. He's seen the sleazy side of town and he knows what it's like living on a battlefield. I'm not getting through to them… I can see it in their faces."

"Maybe you're reading them wrong. If they're from the gutter you should appeal to sentiment. The rich bitch who killed a working man for revenge. The heartless vigilante □ "

"Uh-uh, no way, Jerry!" Abrams interrupted, putting a hand on the desk for support as he stood up abruptly. "For all your blue-collar background that you like to brag about at election time, you sit here so high on Olympus you're more out of touch than I am. The Liberal Hour has come and gone. And the plebs are the most conservative of the lot!"

"So play it the other way," Jerry shot back. "Give 'em the old law-and-order line."

154

"You still don't see it do you?" asked
Abrams, frustrated by Jerry's lack of
helpfulness. "You're average Joe American
is no more into law and order than he's into
social reform. What the people are crying out
for is *justice*, and there's a growing
perception that we're not delivering the
goods."

"Are you sure you're speaking for *them*
Dan?"

Dialogue does not have to be intense. In my second novel, I
developed part of the story at a leisurely pace with a romantic
interlude on a restaurant by the river Thames. In the scene, a private
detective who was hired to find a wealthy man who has since been
found dead is having a candle-lit dinner with the policewoman who
is in charge of the murder investigation (non-dialogue has been cut).

"So where did you get the money to take
women to places like this?"

…

"Who says I take other women to places like
this?"

…

"It must be costing you a fortune even if it's
just me," she said, swallowing a mouthful of
beluga caviar.

…

"Well let's just say that the Digby family
paid me very well, and up front at that!"

As the scene progresses, slowly but surely they talk less about the
case and more about personal matters.

Dialogue also varies according to genre. In a hard-boiled detective
story you might get an exchange like this during a confrontation
between hero and villain:

155

"You've just made the second biggest mistake of your life."

"Oh yeah, what's the biggest?"

"The one you're *about* to make."

You wouldn't of course get an exchange like that in a classic Agatha Christie set at a quiet country house or in a rural village. On the other hand you wouldn't expect to hear people talking about the weather in a gritty tale of American private investigator set in the tough streets of the inner city.

The pitfalls of dialogue

We have seen that dialogue has many strengths. It can be used to characterize individuals or the relationship between two or more. It can evoke the time when the book is set and convey a sense of the local culture and ethos. It can also advance the plot both by providing information to the reader and by informing the characters in the story, thereby prompting them to their next action.

From the point of view of the reader, the main strength of dialogue is that it is easy to follow. The novelist and essayist Gore Vidal once compared dialogue to a series of steps down which the reader could skip at a brisk pace, in contrast to the steep blocks of long narrative.

But dialogue also has potential weaknesses, if it is executed badly. Let us consider, for example, a case in which dialogue is used as a means of conveying information from one character to another. Rather than play fast and lose with the reputation of another writer, I will put my own on the line. Below is a passage of dialogue that does not appear in any book — and is most unlikely to. It is a *rewritten* version of a passage from my fourth book *Reckless Justice*.

The background to the passage is that a man who has been killing off the jurors who wrongly convicted his brother, has engineered a meeting with a woman who was on the jury. She is currently on holiday in Holland. So far he has not killed any of the *women* from the jury, only men. The young woman doesn't know what has been happening to the other jurors, because she has been backpacking in

Europe, and was not following the news in England where the story is set. Consequently, she doesn't realize that he is planning to kill her.

(Sentences other than dialogue have been cut.)

> "It sounds like you were quite a cunning little minx."
>
> "There's an element of truth in that," she said. "But I'd had some rough experiences *outside* the company that brought out the street-fighter in me. You see, just after I decided to stay on, after my first attempt to resign, I was summoned for jury service. And some things happened in that case that made me really angry. It was a complicated case and the charges were quite serious. I mean *very* angry. I wanted to discuss the evidence – *all* the evidence, and not just the part that they cared about.
>
> "That part was the DNA evidence. And it was quite strong. But it wasn't conclusive. It was a matter of statistical probabilities. And most of them didn't understand statistics, let alone genetics. Anyway, they only wanted to look at the DNA evidence. And they didn't even want to *discuss* it. They were so sure it meant that he was guilty that they just wanted to take a vote and convict him. I wanted to discuss it at least. And I wanted to talk about some of the other evidence – like his alibi. His alibi was that he was with his brother. They were playing chess…

One of the many problems with the above passage is that the girl speaks without interruption. Of course to some extent it is inevitable that this particular passage of dialogue will be largely a one-way process: the girl has the information and is passing it on to the man who is – or in this case pretends to be – in a state of ignorance.

But although the conveying of information is a one-way process, the recipient of the information still has a presence which must be

157

represented in the dialogue as it would be in real life. Of course the girl would be very anxious to speak – to get it off her chest. But would the man just sit there in silence, letting her talk. And note how she seems to anticipate all the questions that he would ask in real life? Is that realistic? Clearly not.

So how the should the passage be written? This is how it appeared in the book (and it is only marginally better).

> "It sounds like you were quite a cunning little minx."
>
> "There's an element of truth in that," she said. "But I'd had some rough experiences *outside* the company that brought out the street-fighter in me."
>
> "What experiences?"
>
> "Just after I decided to stay on, after my first attempt to resign, I was summoned for jury service."
>
> "And?"
>
> "Some things happened in that case that made me really angry. I mean *very* angry."
>
> "Like what?"
>
> "It was a complicated case and the charges were quite serious. I wanted to discuss the evidence – *all* the evidence, and not just the parts that they cared about."
>
> "I don't understand."
>
> "There was DNA evidence. And it was quite strong. But it wasn't conclusive. It was all a matter of statistical probabilities. And most of them didn't understand the statistics, let alone genetics. Anyway, they only wanted to look at the DNA evidence. And they didn't even want to *discuss* it. They were so sure it meant that he was guilty that they just wanted to take a vote and convict him. I wanted to discuss it at least. And I wanted to talk about some of the other evidence."

"Like what?"

"Like the fact that he had an *alibi*."

"An alibi?"

"Yes. His alibi was that he was with his brother. They were playing chess…"

In the second version, we hear the speech of the apparently better informed party punctuated by questions from the other, giving it a more natural ring and making it easier to follow. These are the questions that the reader would want to ask. The less-informed party thus stands in for the reader, as well as having a role in the drama. (In fact, the less-well informed party was not really less-informed at all. But in the context of the thriller he was posing as such for his own reasons.)

Another problem that can occur in dialogue is confusion on the part of the reader as to who is speaking. This problem is particularly acute with long blocks of dialogue.

There is also a danger of subjects slipping "out of character". Finally, dialogue can suffer from the tendency to "tell" important information rather than show it, in breach of one of the cardinal rules of good literature. When writing dialogue, take advantage of its strengths, but try to avoid the pitfalls.

Chapter 8 – How do I create realistic characters?

What is "characterization"?

In real life it is possible to know a person for many years and still not to really know them. That may or may not be acceptable, depending on ones relationship with the other person, but in *can* happen. But in literature and drama, it is unacceptable. If the reader fails to understand at least the central characters of the story, then the writer has failed in one of his principal duties. One could argue that in some cases the reader might be exceptionally obtuse. But in literature – as in the retail business – the customer is always right. And in literature the customer is the *reader*.

In order for literature and drama to work, we have to understand the people we are reading about or watching. This doesn't necessarily have to happen when he characters are first introduced – indeed, it may be useful in some novels to conceal the true nature of a character for much of the story. But in the end we must understand the characters, or it has been a wasted endeavor for writer and reader alike.

Even where a character's true nature is concealed, we should know enough about that person that we recognize – with hindsight – that we *should* have seen it coming. Furthermore, when we read about characters, their actions should consistently reflect the type of person they are in order for them to be believable. This does not mean that they necessarily have to remain unchanged throughout the story. Characters after all do change. And if a story is about momentous events, or even just *significant* events, then it is only natural that they *should* change.

Change in character can be a major aspect of a story. The person who appears at first to be a quiet little mouse may turn into a lion as the story unfolds. Or characters may learn something about their faults and correct them. But character change must be driven by a *reason*.

This is characterization: presenting to the reader with enough facts for them to understand who and what the characters are. And because the reader hasn't got much time in which to go through this learning process, we must distill these facts into a concentrated essence that can be served up to the reader and consumed by them as they read.

At the same time, this essence must be easy to swallow, not so concentrated that the character becomes a caricature. Getting the concentration right, and serving it in the right size sips, demands great skill and is one of the most important tests of ability that the writer faces. Characterization, in literature, uses a complex tool-set consisting of dialogue, narrative and descriptive writing. It is an art that separates not only bad writers from good ones, but also good writers from great ones.

The author Michael Crichton famously dismissed characterization, or at least relegated it to the back burner. Crichton could get away with it. His books were in many respects exciting and action-packed. But if you aspire to be a successful writer, do not dismiss characterization out of hand.

What we need to know about a character

Obviously we need to know enough about a character to believe that he or she is real – to see them as three-dimensional human beings. This does not mean that they have to be ordinary. Exceptional human beings exist too. And of course one of the recurring themes in many a great book is how ordinary people rise above themselves in extraordinary circumstances. The "Winston Smith" character of George Orwell's *1984* and the "Jefferson Smith" of Frank Capra's film *Mr Smith Goes to Washington* are both examples of this symbolic synthesis of greatness and ordinariness. This is even expressed in their names. Thus Jefferson Smith, gets his first name, from founding father Thomas Jefferson. Winston Smith derives his first name from the British Prime Minister during World War 2 –

Winston Churchill. The Smith in both their names, links them to the ordinary man, by using the most common surname of English-speaking countries.

We do not of course need to know *everything* about a character, just enough to make the character's actions intelligible to the audience. In the last module we saw in an example from my book *A Fool for a Client* how Justine was presented as a tough-minded character right from the beginning. If she wasn't as tenacious and single-minded as she was portrayed, none of her actions would have made sense. Both her insistence on conducting her own defense and her other actions in the story were dependent on that consistent characterization.

According to Ralph Waldo Emerson, "a foolish consistency is the hobgoblin of little minds." But consistency is the staple of good literature. Even when a character is duplicitous and hypocritical, there should be some internal consistency in their character. A meticulously careful person who commits a casual error when committing what is intended to be the perfect murder is an example of bad characterization. On the other hand, a meticulously careful murderer who makes the kind of error that a meticulous person might make (like going back to straighten something out on the writing bureau out of his sense of tidiness, for example), is an example of *good* characterization. Thus a clue to the meticulous nature of the murderer at the crime scene, that serves as a pointer to the killer's identity, is a credible literary device, where a stupid (and thus unbelievable error) by such a killer would be a constructional flaw.

In this regard it is important to remember that characterization isn't just to make the reader feel comfortable and at home with the characters, but also to advance the plot as a whole.

What motivates characters?

Before we can present good characterization of our characters we have to plan them. And in order to plan them we need first to understand them ourselves. Obviously a good starting point for understanding a person is identifying what motivates them. People are motivated by a whole variety of factors and it is the relative strength of these factors that motivates them in a given situation.

Below is a list of some of the factors that motivate people:

- Envy/jealousy
- Greed/avarice
- Justice (vengeance for an objective wrong)
- Vengeance (for a subjective wrong)
- Sympathy/pity
- Guilt/remorse
- Pride
- Love
- Lust
- Fear
- Friendship
- Loneliness

The reader would be excused for thinking that this is just an expanded list of the seven deadly sins, with a few other characteristics thrown in for good measure. Certainly most of the deadly sins are to be found on that list either in their original form or some variant thereof (e.g. read "anger" for vengeance). However, the fact remains that people are motivated by their emotions ("motivated" and "emotion" even share a common root). This motivation includes both positive and negative emotions. And of course not everyone will agree on which emotions are negative.

How might these emotions translate into characterizations that can move a story?

Envy or jealousy might prompt some one to murder, to theft or to the making of false accusations. These might be against a more successful colleague, a rival in matters of love or a wealthy neighbor or relative. Alternatively such envy might simply strain the relationship of former friends.

There is of course some overlap with other motivating factors here. Greed/avarice might also prompt theft. Vengeance might manifest

163

itself in the murder of a love rival or false accusation against a more successful colleague. And of course the same greed that might manifest itself in theft, might almost express itself as ruthlessness in business – depending on other aspects of the character's nature.

And of course, one person's actions can have a ripple effect on others: one character acting on his motives creates further motives in others who act on them. The greedy man's business success might involve trampling over another, who in turn ants revenge. Consequently, a story is propelled by its highly motivated characters – the greater the motivation, the faster and more extreme the propulsion.

There are numerous combinations of motives that may apply to a single character and numerous combinations of characters. George Polti's great work *The Thirty Six Dramatic Situations*, classifies 36 basic plots (and sub-categories of them) stating succinctly which type of characters are in them. These characters are defined in terms like "an ambitious person", "a superior rival", "an unfortunate" "the cause or the author of the mistake", etc. These are not in themselves characterizations, but rather index card headings of characterizations to be fleshed out by the writer.

One does not of course have to read this work, to have the inspiration to populate ones story. Any person with a bit of imagination can come up with a collection of characters and emotions. The great challenge to the writer is to convey these motivations to the reader in a way that is intelligible and coherent. For writers who want to appeal to the modern – impatient – reader, there is the added challenge of conveying the motivations in a way that does not hold up the story. Modern readers want characters to make sense (internal logic) but are not interested in character studies. They want *action* by characters, not characters who occasionally act.

What the writer has to do therefore is *not* merely decide what his characters *are*, but also use his literary tools to *convey this information to the reader*.

Tools of characterization

We have seen, in Chapters 5, 6 and 7, that the main tools of the writer are description, narration and dialogue. Those chapters showed you how to use these tools, and how their respective techniques could be used to convey to the readers the nature of your characters. It is perhaps worth recapping their roles in relation to characterization, specifically.

Description

For the purpose of advancing the plot, narration and dialogue are the principle tools, with description running a distant third. But when it comes to characterization, description comes into its own. It never supplants or even equals dialogue and narration, even in this area. But it does rise considerably in importance.

Description can include a person's natural appearance, how they groom their appearance, clothing and the places where they live. When the story – or any part of it – is written in the first person or third person subjective, one can add to this list what the person notices, as this too can show what kind of a person they are. We saw in Chapter 5 several examples of a description described from a character's point of view which gave us as much insight into the observer as the thing being observed. This is a powerful method and one that is well worth using if your book is written from any but the third-person-objective viewpoint.

An important point to bear in mind, when looking at the list of descriptive items that *can* be used to develop a character, is that not all of these devices *must* or even *should* be used. Even in the case of a major character, the description should not be overloaded. The writer should be selective and try to determine how much description is necessary.

Remember also that even if you see your character in a particular way, the reader does not necessarily *have* to see them in the same way. If it is merely a writer's preference, rather than a constructional necessity, then you do not necessarily have to leave it in.

There are usually several different ways of saying the same thing about a character. For example, if you want to show that a character is vain and obsessed with his appearance, you might describe him wearing his immaculate shirt and neatly pressed trousers. You might observe that exactly half an inch of shirt extends from the cuffs of his Armani suit. Or you could describe him grooming himself in front of the mirror as he prepares to go out. This last approach, however, takes the technique out of the real of description and into the realm of...

Narrative writing

A far more important tool of characterization is the narrative technique. Characters are defined principally by what they *do*. It is very easy to *tell* the reader that the hero is brave, but unless the story actually *shows* him doing something brave, the writer's effort is meaningless. And brave need not of course mean foolish or reckless. Naturally, the critical time for the hero to be brave is at the climax of the story, when his heroism is called upon to save the day. But it might also be a good idea to prepare the reader for this along the way.

Suppose for example, the hero of the story is a seemingly wimp-ish character, with a hero inside him struggling to get out. We may wish to show his heroic side later as part of the story. We don't wish to give too much away at the beginning. But when he does prove himself to be a hero, we want the audience to believe it. We don't want them to say "oh he'd never do that!"

So we have to set him up as a character who *might* do that, without making it obvious that he would. For this we might create an example of mini-heroism that suggests his heroic qualities without piling in on too thick. For example we might have him hearing an argument between a man and a woman and pausing, pretending to tie his shoelaces just in case the argument develops into more than that and he needs to intervene. This gets the balance right, because we don't actually know if he *would* have the courage to intervene. But we know that he *wants* to, and at least he isn't just walking on and ignoring the situation as others might.

166

If we want an alternative, more sentimental example, we could have him climbing up a lamp-post to rescue a stranded cat. Afterwards we could have him walking away shaking, telling the reader that he was afraid of heights. This should show that he is a man who is not without fears but who *overcomes* those fears – the hallmark of a *true hero*.

In either of these two examples, when his real heroism kicks in, during the climax or later phases of the story, it is not an anomaly to the reader's mind, because the reader has already been prepared for it. The same principle of advance preparation applies of course to the villain.

Suppose, for example, our villain is a nasty, petty, small-minded and malicious individual. And suppose further that our story is a mystery. We obviously don't want the villain to be recognized as what he is before the denouement. But on the other hand, we don't want the readers to disbelieve it when the villain is unveiled for what he is. Indeed, we want the readers to thump the side of the heads and shriek "Of course!" So we have to set it up in such a way as to prepare the ground without rubbing the reader's face in it.

We could have the villain do something like kick the dog or not leave the waiter a tip or slam the phone down in anger. None of these would conclusively reveal the character as a villain. Indeed many of us could do some of those things. But if we string several of them together at suitable intervals, interspersed with other events involving other characters, we can prepare the reader for the surprise without actually telegraphing it.

This does not mean that as the writer you should go out of your way to create characterizing incidents. Rather it means that, when writing, you should be aware that the incidents you create will reflect the nature of your characters and should be consistent with what you intend the characters to be.

There are countless ways of hinting at a character with simple little episodes of incidents. If you want to convey the fact that a character is a miser, it is far better to have him choosing the cheapest item on the menu at a restaurant that is modestly priced to begin with, than

167

simply telling the reader that "He was a miser." If you want the reader to recognize him as gullible, it makes more sense to have him repeating an obviously bogus urban myth or paying money to a workman who has just exaggerated the amount of work done, than merely *telling* the reader that "he was a trifle gullible at times."

Dialogue

The final weapon in the armory of characterization is of, course, dialogue. This means not just the content of what people say but also how they say it and what others say about them. Here's an example from my thriller *Reckless Justice*, in which I introduce a minor, but not completely insignificant, character. The passage contains narrative and descriptive writing, as well as dialogue. But it is the dialogue that is most telling.

> "Tell your sister to put some fuckin' clothes on!" yelled Billy Lewis as he passed Sandra, his younger daughter, at the bottom of the staircase. He grabbed the newspaper from the letter box and stomped his way into the kitchen, leaving a trail of marks from his dirty slippers on the already dirty lino floor.
>
> "How do you want your eggs?" asked his wife timidly, barely turning from the frying pan on the oil-encrusted hob. She looked briefly, with disgust, at the pot-bellied man in the string vest. But the disgust was with herself.
>
> "Like I always 'ave 'em," he snarled, opening his morning tabloid and flicking through to the sports section. "Wright's got injured again," he said, not really caring if she was interested.
>
> "What's that?"
>
> "Ian Wright. Injured 'is fuckin' ankle."
>
> "That's a pity."
>
> "Bloody right it's a pity. Their only one point ahead of United and there's a still a couple

more games to play! Where's my fuckin' toast?"

She took the toast from the toaster and put it in front of him. Then she rushed back to the frying pan to stop his eggs sticking.

"It's cold."

"What?" asked his wife.

"The toast."

"I'm sorry," she said, rushing to the toaster red-faced and throwing in two more slices of white bread. "I'll make you some more."

The passage illustrates the nature of the two characters at several levels. Billy's use of expletives shows his boorishness, vulgarity and (at the risk of snobbery) low breeding. His aggressive snarling indicates his bullying nature. His wife's self-effacing manner indicates not love but fear – further enhancing Billy's bullying image. Later we learn that he was a juror who bullied other jurors into returning a verdict of guilty in a highly contentious murder case. When we get to that phase of the story, we can believe it because we have already seen what sort of a person he is.

Heroes

By and large the most important character in any story is the hero or heroine. Occasionally there are stories in which the villain is the most important character. If one thinks of Hannibal Lector as the villain, then this applies to Thomas Harris's *Silence of the Lambs*. More on this later.

Different heroes for different genres

Obviously different types of story call for heroes that are appropriate to the genre. The hero or heroine of an old-style Agatha Christie story set in a quiet country mansion or a picturesque village could be the local vicar or librarian. (Actually, so could the villain!) On the other hand if your book is a police investigative thriller, the most logical hero would be a police officer. In a hard-boiled thriller or *roman noire* the hero could be a private investigator or a cop, but is always expected to be tough. In the old days, these heroes were almost exclusively male. But these days that rule is hopelessly out of date.

Clearly the genre places a limit on what type of person the hero or heroine may be. But this does not mean that the role is confined to a single particular type, let alone a stereotype. For example in a legal drama the hero(ine) doesn't have to be a lawyer. It can be a young paralegal, a private detective hired by one of the lawyers, an inquisitive juror or even the judge. Each of these offers a different perspective.

If the hero is a young paralegal, the story can be a rites-of-passage story about youthful ideals meeting the harsh realities of the adult world. If the hero is a judge, it can be a story about a wise observer who thinks he/she has seen everything, finding out that there *is* something new under the sun. Or alternatively the judge might be some one who has spent their professional life in the front row seat of a passive spectator who decides, for once in his life, to play the role of leading actor. This might entail going out onto the streets and investigating at great risk to their professional career and even his life.

The private detective angle is fairly conventional character *type* to have in a thriller, be it legal or hard-boiled. But this does not mean he has to be a conventional *character*. But he or she should have the kind of characteristics – or background – that would cause a person to become a private detective. This might be inquisitiveness, a former police background, being a failed lawyer (or the black sheep of a legal family) or even an unemployed person applying for a job and stumbling into the profession.

But the choice of hero or heroine is broader than these well-worn types. A scientist or businessman, a politician or civil servant, a soldier or military correspondent, an office drone or window cleaner – these are just some of the possibilities that these diverse genres offer for the creative writer. Thus the genre is a guide rail to the character of the hero, but not a straitjacket.

What motivates him or her?

As noted above, this is an important question to be asked with *any* character. But it assumes a greater importance with the hero or heroine. Of course the obvious answers are things like: "a desire to know the truth" "a quest for love" or "a passion for justice." But these are just the obvious motivations that drive the hero through the story as a whole. There are usually more subtle factors as well that drive subplots or particular episodes within the story as a whole.

And motives imply prior causes. If someone is envious, then what are they invoice of? If a character feels guilt about something then what was the cause of the guilt? If they love an unlikely person, then thee must be some reason for that unlikely love. This leads to the question of background. Major characters should have some background – especially the hero/heroine and the villain. Even if the writer wants to create a particularly enigmatic hero, some thought should be given to the hero's background. This doesn't mean that the writer must supply a potted biography for the reader to digest at the beginning, nor even necessarily draw one up for reference purposes. All it means is that you as the writer must be *conscious of the fact* that your character has a past. He may have sprung from your imagination. But for your readers he is of woman born and did not arrive out of nowhere.

As with so many things in writing, there is no rigid rule about how much of the hero the writer should reveal. But it is imperative that you understand your hero. Is he a perfectionist or one who will settle for second best? Is he an idealist, a realist or a cynic?

In Nelson de Mille's *Word of Honor*, a business executive and former US army officer in Vietnam has been accused in a non-fiction book of ordering his platoon to carry out a massacre. As a result of this accusation, and the publicity given to it, he is recalled into service □ choosing not to fight his recall in the civilian courts – and then court-martialled. What then is his motivation for not fighting his recall?

At one level he is apparently motivated by a desire to clear his name. But at another level he is struggling to lay to rest the demon's of the past. This presents itself as a paradox. Because the reason he still has these demons is because he has not confronted the issue until now. For example, he has never told his wife about it. This is not altogether surprising, as his wife is a former anti-Vietnam war activist. Nevertheless it means that he has never been able to speak about it to the one person who might have been able to ease the burden on his conscience.

Instead he has tried to put it behind him by bottling it up. So it is really a story about a man struggling to forget a painful past but finding out in the end that he cannot simply forget and must confront the past instead.

In Joseph diMona's *Last Man at Arlington*, the hero is a justice department lawyer trying to track down an assassin who has threatened to kill six named people. One of the six is the hero himself and another of whom is the hero's ex-girlfriend. (They met as White House interns during the Kennedy Administration.) At the superficial level, the hero's motivation is a desire to protect the innocent, including a woman for whom he still feels some affection. But at another level he is a man grappling with the disillusion and cynicism that set in after the Kennedy assassination.

In Jeffrey Archer's *Not a Penny More, Not a Penny Less*, the plot is about four men who have been swindled by a confidence trickster into making a bad investment out of which the con-man has profited. The four men set about devising a series of schemes to regain the money. The hero of the book is one of these four men,

Superficially, this isn't even about revenge or retribution, but simply about debt recovery. However the hero is motivated not only by wish to get his money back, but also by a desire to prove that he isn't a loser □ as he has been until now. His motivation is thus one of self-assertion and regaining his pride and self-respect.

Escaping the past? Recapturing lost ideals? Asserting oneself? These are just a small sample of the motivations behind the heroes of stories. Such factors may of course be present in other characters besides heroes. But it is in the hero that they assume special importance.

Level and placement of detail?

Two questions pose themselves to the writer when it comes to deciding how much character detail to present to the reader. How much? And where to place it?

The question of how much character detail is an important one. A novel is not a character study – except perhaps in the hands of a great writer like Dosteyevsky. A novel is principally a story with *events*. The hero should *have* a character, but the writer should not dwell on it. The story should *move* with the character, not stand still and look at him. (This is to some extent analogous to the Homeric method of narrative description.)

To some extent, the question of how much detail can only be answered when the process of writing gets underway. You can plan the hero's background in great detail before you start writing, or you can wait until the creative juices flow and then start thinking about these issues as the narrative unfolds on the paper (or screen) before you. You may find that you have planned far more detail than you can ever put in. If you are writing a short book, you might find that too much character detail slows down your story. On the other hand if you are writing or planning a long book then you may find that action alone is not enough and your readers will *want* to know more about your central character.

So how much detail about the hero should the writer include? Obviously more information should be given about the hero than about a minor character. But how big is big, goes the old cliché. One of the factors that determines how much detail to provide is whether the hero is a one-off or a recurring character in a series of books. If the latter, then you might like to pace the detail and revelations. For example, you might like to mention his military past in the first book and then give a brief flashback to one of his military adventures in the next. Then again, the event of the earlier book will *themselves* form part of his past in the subsequent books.

The golden rule is never forget that the book isn't usually about who the hero *is*; it's about that he *does*. After all, it's what he *does* that makes him the hero!

The related question is *where* to place the detail. By and large it is best to intersperse the detail throughout the story. In my second book, *The Other Victim*, part of the background of Emmett Freeman, the hero, was that he had got his first degree in physics and wanted to be a theoretical physicist but was falsely accused of cheating on his final exams and found guilty by an internal review board. I got the idea from this from a newspaper story about a math student who had suffered the same fate on the basis that the examiner had used an unusual method of calculation in his model solutions and the student had repeated the examiner's mistakes. The committee concluded that he could only have written these identical results if he had had prior access to the examiner's model solutions to the problems. (Of course, how he would *remember* such solutions they didn't explain.)

In the course of my book, I first revealed, in one section of dialogue between the hero and the son of a missing billionaire that the hero is looking for, how the hero set himself up in business as a consultant by challenging the patent applications of big companies and effectively blackmailing them into hiring him as a consultant. Later on, during a romantic candle-lit dinner with the heroine (an ambitious and intelligent police woman) in a restaurant overlooking the Thames, he tells her how he moved from science to law in an effort to clear his name. It turned out that in fact the examiner had copied from the hero – using the hero's answers as model solutions after realizing that his own model solutions were full of error.

Whilst I revealed this about half way through the book in the dialogue between the hero and the heroine, I had already hinted at it with various remarks and asides interspersed throughout the dialogue in the earlier phases of the book. The important thing was that I had *planned* the background and knew it, so when it came to writing, I was free to decide as I went along where to place these details. In effect I could drop in hints and clues as I felt they were called for, based on my own prior knowledge.

In this sense there is a definite advantage to prior planning before writing a book. But not all writers like to work this way. Some are more comfortable starting out with just a beginning and an end – deciding on the middle along the way. At any rate, if you do get a latent idea, don't shy away from incorporating it into your work, even if you have to go back and do a lot of re-writing to make it fit. (That's why word processors and computers were invented after all.)

For example, in the same book that I have just been speaking about, I decided – about a third of the way through the book – to change the heroine from an investigative reporter into a police woman. I did this because I felt that this would give her a more central and direct role in the case and also because it would put her on a stronger footing vis-à-vis the hero. But this meant that whole large chunks of what I had already written had to be scrapped and new passages written in their place!

If you are planning to write a series of books around the same hero or heroine, it is advisable to plan the character and their background in even greater detail than for a long single book. However, you do not have to reveal all of this information in the first book. The revelations can be paced across the entire series.

There should of course be enough material in the first book to make the character intelligible to the reader. If he is a divorced ex-military policeman for example, this should go into the first book. But you can save up little episodes with his wife or army career for later books to insert as flashbacks as and when appropriate and relevant to the story.

Role model or feet of clay?

Perhaps one of the most contentious questions in writing thrillers is whether the hero showed be a model of perfection for the viewer to aspire to (if not emulate) or a flawed hero with weaknesses and imperfections.

The Russian-born American writer Ayn Rand was a firm believer in role-model heroes. She cited the example of James Bond (from the books, not the movies) as an archetype or the sort of hero that writers should aspire to create and readers should aspire to be. In her non-fiction book *The Romantic Manifesto*, in which she stated her artistic credo, she extolled this type of hero and claimed that everyone (except the most morally depraved) would wish to be like James Bond. She dismissed the description of this kind of thriller as "Escapism" regarding it as pejorative. Instead she described the genre as "Romantic Symbolism" in contrast to her own books like *The Fountainhead* and *Atlas Shrugged* which she regarded as Romantic Realism. (She was using the word "romantic" in the 19th century sense of the word.)

An alternative school of thought holds that writers should put a little bit of good in their bad characters and a bit of bad in their good characters. This is a bit like the famous oriental yin/yang symbol. Not only do the two light and dark images complement each other in their intertwined shape, but there is a little small black circle in the white area and a small white circle in the black area to show that there is a little bit on yin in yang and a bit of yang in yin.

Under this literary philosophy, it is quite legitimate for the hero to have feet of clay and for the villain to have redeeming features. Strictly speaking the two are separate issues. Many a writer with strong views about right and wrong will be happy to give their villains redeeming features so as to make them more three-dimensional, but would balk at the prospect of diluting the moral purity of the hero. Ayn Rand, for example would be turning in her grave at the thought of it.

On the other hand, this was an ethical issue more than an aesthetic one. For some one who had such strong views as Ayn Rand, it would have made no sense to create a hero who was ethically contaminated (although some of her heroes had self-doubt). But not every reader has the same ethical code. And not every writer need have the same aesthetic

In my thriller *Reckless Justice* for example, the hero was a vigilante who was taking the law into his own hands by killing (some of) the jurors who had found his brother guilty of murder. This sort of story, in which the hero defies the widely-held conventions of society, is a risky area to get into, and writers should only buck the trend of the accepted ethics of thrillers if they feel particularly strongly about it.

Less risky and more common is the hero who has weakness of the flesh rather than a tendency towards serious crime against his neighbor. Sherlock Holmes was an addict of opium derivative drugs, while many a hard-boiled hero has an intimate relationship with the liquor bottle. The forensic psychologist Fitz in the TV series *Cracker* has problems keeping his vows of marital fidelity in addition to his love-fest with the bottle. He is perhaps a hero for our times, in which such weaknesses are seen as the rule rather than the exception. And if normal people are like that, why shouldn't he be?

This is an area of choice which the writer has to make. The important thing to remember is that there is no hard and fast rule about a hero's ethics. There are only the guiding principles that the hero should be interesting, consistent (this does not rule out character change as the story progresses) and should be presented in a way that is intelligible to the reader. Finally the hero should fit in naturally and plausibly with the story. Whether you start off with the character and create the plot around him or start off with a plot and populate it with the characters that drive it, the hero and the story in which he exists should fit together. A hard-boiled country vicar, or a sensitive and frail city cop who quotes the psalms, generally won't cut it - unless the genre is comedy!

Hero's side kick

Not every hero has a sidekick, but when he does, the side-kick is a major character, although not quite on a par with the hero in terms of importance. Nevertheless, he is important for a number of reasons. Firstly he is very often the sounding board for the hero (and vice versa). He is the voice of the curious reader, asking the hero all the questions that the reader would like to ask.

177

A rule of thumb formulated by Robert Knox in his preface to *Best Detective Stories of 1928-29* is that the side-kick's intelligence should be slightly below that of the average reader. Although Knox wrote this rule along with nine others in what he called a "Decalogue", it is not actually written in stone. You, as a writer, are free to make the side-kick more than averagely dumb or you can make him intelligent but more approachable than the hero.

As mentioned earlier, part of the role of the side-kick in a thriller is to reveal clues to the reader, so as to be fair to the reader, while at the same time not giving the game away. This important function means that the side-kick is usually an ever-present character – at least in those scenes where the hero appears. But in terms of characterization, the side-kick need not be all that important. If the side-kick is the narrator, it is more important for the side-kick to tell us about the hero than to tell us about himself or herself.

Thus we have the paradox that the side-kick is important but does not require heavy characterization. But of course if the side-kick is telling the story then the reader must identify with him and empathize with him? How do we resolve the paradox. The most effective way is to let the side-kick reveal himself in little tidbits of dialogue and asides. Bit by bit we will learn about the side-kick, but never at the expense of the hero. Indeed. Very often, the most important event in the side-kick's background – as far as the reader is concerned – is how and when he first met the hero.

One final point to bear in mind is that the side-kick is such an old and venerable institution that the inclusion of a side-kick, let alone a side-kick/narrator runs the risk of characterizing the genre as old-fashioned.

Villains

The same questions that apply to the hero or heroine also apply to the villain, although they answers are usually very different. We need to know what motivates him or her. We need to know if they have any redeeming features. We may also want to know how they became what they became – that issue of background again.

In some stories, the villain is not important at all. Indeed, a draft screenplay of my published thriller *Tarnished Heroes* was criticized on the grounds that the villain was "not particularly memorable." This was undeniably the truth, although not necessarily an indictment of the work. The villain was not intended to be memorable because the theme of the book was the character conflicts inside the hero's own psyche. However a spate of films shortly prior to that – like *Silence of the Lambs* and *Seven* – had conditioned viewers to *expect* memorable villains with characterizations at least as highly developed as the hero or heroine. At least this is the case if the villain is a serial killer.

This wasn't always the case. The serial murderer in the Clint Eastwood film *Dirty Harry* was not particularly memorable (apart from his face). Even in *Silence of the Lambs*, the serial killer they were trying to catch, "Buffalo Bill" was never really developed to any particular depth. It is the *other* villain – Hannibal Lecter – whom we all remember.

Nevertheless, the fact remains that at the time of writing there is a demand for memorable villains, and it is up to the writer to decide whether to buck the trend or ride with it. If you, as a writer want to create a memorable villain, there is no reason ethically or aesthetically why you should not do so. On the other hand, you may prefer to focus on your hero and keep your villain's soul in the shadows. Be that as it may, villains do require *some* characterization.

What motivates him/her?

As stated above, the same basic question applies to the villain as to the hero, but usually with a different answer. Is the villain motivated by greed? By lust? By envy? By vengeance? By pride? These of course are the factors that are likely to motivate the villain in his or her villainy. And there may be a combination of more than one factor.

To some extent, these motivational factors might flow naturally from the plot. But you may still wish to develop them in the story. If the villain has killed a rival to obtain promotion, you might want to show the villain's ambitiousness. Or you might present the villain as a timid, mousy, "Uriah Heap" like character, masquerading as a humble figure who is content to be out of the limelight. But then you might drop a few hints that he is resentful of this role or his superiors. Or perhaps you fear that such hints might telegraph the twist at the end. So instead you adopt a more subtle approach, showing how he really *has* been badly treated by his superiors, to show that he *ought* to feel resentment, even if he doesn't.

Then again, perhaps you can reduce the danger of telegraphing the ending my making it seem at first as if he is a genuinely insignificant figure who hasn't really done much for the company. Thereafter, you can use the "onion-skin" approach to factual revelation, peeling off layer after layer to show that he has actually done a lot for the company but that it was not appreciated. You might do this in the context of showing how other living characters in the story (not the victim) stole the credit for his achievements. This would appear to mark *them* out as excessively ambitious and thus might create a few red herrings. For instance, what if it is shown that the timid person who turns out to be the villain has had his ideas stolen by a *paranoid superior* colleague who outranks the victim in the organization. This could be presented in such a way as to suggest that the high-ranking plagiarist felt threatened by the fast promotion of a dead rival but not by the timid subordinate from whom he stole certain ideas. Then it is this *paranoid superior* who appears to be the murderer and he becomes the prime suspect in the minds of the readers.

This is just one example of the way that you can slip in your characterization in such a way as to make the denouement credible, without giving away too much too soon.

Degrees of Evil (those redeeming features!)

As with heroes we come across the question of mixing vice with virtue. In literature as in life, there are degrees of evil. So one of the questions you will have to decide is how villainous to make your villains. In general it is considered more acceptable to give your villains redeeming features than to give the hero feet of clay.

But when is it appropriate to do so? A simple rule might be that it should vary according to the severity of the crime. Thus it might be all right to give a burglar or a thief redeeming features but not a murderer. But what if the murderer was provoked? What if it the murderer kills another murderer?

All right, you might say, there are some circumstances in which a murderer might have redeeming features, but never a rapist. On the other hand there was an episode of the TV series *Cracker* in which a rapist – although portrayed as being vicious in the commission of his crimes – was also presented as a tormented figure whose childhood torment had turned him into what he became.

All right, you might respond, but a tormented figure still isn't he same thing as a sympathetic one. Fair enough, but in my own thriller *No Way Out,* I presented an "Eldridge Cleaver" type character – a former rapist, now repentant for his past – whose past had caught up with him as he found himself accused of another rape in a finely balanced legal thriller. Perhaps most importantly, the reason he had become a rapist (in the story) was a mixture of political and personal: his mother had been raped in front of him as a child by white racist cops and he was trying to get revenge on what he saw as the "white establishment".

Perhaps, this is not a good example either, as this character was not presented explicitly as the villain of the story. But this is itself highly controversial. It serves to illustrate that it is possible to defy convention and political correctness. Writing controversial material is always risky: controversy doesn't always sell, whatever the advertising industry says. But it can if it is not overdone.

How powerful/clever should the villain be?

In order for the hero to be tested, the villain must be a worthy adversary. Without this the story has no tension for the reader. If the story is a mystery, then the villain should be clever. If the story is one of suspense, then the villain should be powerful in some way.

"Power" can of course mean many things. He might be *physically strong*. He might be *weak but ruthless*, or even *psychopathic*. He might have as little concern for his own safety as for the well-being of others. This makes him a particularly dangerous opponent, because he is not subject to the usual deterrent factors. Then again he could simply be a *crime lord* with a large, well-armed gang under his control. Or he could be a *captain of industry*. Perhaps he is a *police officer* or a *crooked lawyer or judge*. Maybe he is a *corrupt politician*.

If the story is a mystery then he must be clever enough to stay one-step ahead of the hero for most of the story. Maybe he is an ex-cop who knows all the techniques of criminal investigation. Maybe he is some one on the inside who can keep tabs on the whole process of investigation in which he is being hunted. He could be a scientist or engineer or computer hacker who can keep tabs on his opponents using online resources.

But whatever form his power or cleverness takes, it must be enough to stand as an obstruction between the hero and the hero's goal. If the hero's goal is justice then the villain must have the means to impede his progress towards that goal whether by force or guile.

How much <u>attention</u> to give the villain?

We now return to the question that we first confronted at the start of this section. If your story started from an idea about the villain, then it follows that you will want to put in a lot of information about that villain because of his importance to your thought processes. But if your starting point was the hero or elements of the plot then the amount of detail you need to include about the villain is dictated by that plot. You want the reader to understand the villain and you want the story to move at a reasonable pace. The best test to apply to any piece of data that you want to reveal about the villain is: does it fit? If you have to struggle to find a place or way to include it, that is the surest sign that it doesn't belong there. This also applies to…

Minor characters

Why they are there

A purist would argue that there are no minor characters. If they play a role in the story then they are not minor. If they play no rule in the story then they shouldn't be there. But this is a rather Olympian kind of purity. In a constructional sense a minor character is one who supports the story in an essential sense but whose role only requires a small amount of space in the book to narrate. They are major in the sense that the plot requires their presence and actions. They are minor in the sense that the author doesn't have to give as much thought to them as to the hero and villain (and in some cases the secondary hero or villain).

How much detail?

Because they appear for less time and occupy less space, they do not require such detailed characterization. Any attempt to go into their backgrounds or psychological makeup would simply slow the story down for the reader. There is also a danger that they might eclipse the major characters. If you find a character growing like this then there are two remedies. One is to cut some of the material relating to him. The other is to recognize that he has *become* a major character and write (or rewrite) the story accordingly.

A final point to remember is that where a series of books is planned, there is the possibility that a minor character from one book could become a major character in one more others. For example, in John le Carré's *The Spy Whom Came In From The Cold*, there is a brief reference to a walk-on character called George Smiley who goes on to become the major character in several other of le Carré's books. Worth remembering!

Chapter 9 – How do I begin my novel?

The beginning and ending of a book are both important. According to one venerable cliché of the publishing industry: "The beginning sells your book; the ending sells your *next* book." But does that mean that beginning and ending each have only have one purpose? And how does one go about writing the beginning of a book… or the ending? Let us begin at the beginning.

Uses for the beginning

The beginning serves several purposes. It is used to grab the reader's attention. It can also be used to set the stage for the story. It can be used to introduce the hero or the villain. It can even be used for establishing the genre in the reader's mind, although this is usually a by-product of a good beginning rather than a principal purpose.

Grabbing the reader's attention

The most obvious purpose of the beginning is to grab the reader's attention. Strictly speaking, this is an over-rated function, as people usually decide to buy the book on a basis of the blurb, word-of-mouth recommendation or the reviews (either the reviews quoted on the cover, or reviews that they have read in the press). If the reader *does* open the book in the shop and starts reading from it, the chances are it will be from the *middle* of the book, not the beginning.

Nevertheless, as the publisher's cliché above suggests, the beginning of the book is very important for capturing the attention of an editor at a publishing house. And in the age of self-published eBooks – Amazon and others offer a look inside feature that enables the reader to read the *beginning* of the book. So this is your first – possibly *only* – chance to grab the reader. So make the most of it.

How then might one begin a book in such a way as to grab the reader's attention? Here's an example of how it might be done in a single sentence.

> It is cold at 6:40 in the morning of a March
> day in Paris, and seems even colder when a
> man is about to be executed by firing squad.

The book is *The Day of the Jackal* by Frederick Forsyth.

Written in the present tense (unlike the rest of the book), there is no
questioning the power of that beginning. It would be hard for anyone
not to read on after an opening sentence like that — at least until the
end of the page or chapter. But *why* is it so powerful. Well let us ask
the question another way. What do we feel when we read it? What *I*
felt was an intense desire to know was who *is* this man and why is he
about to be executed? This is presumably just what Frederick
Forsyth intended.

Of course, we soon learn that he was a military officer who was part
of a plot to assassinate General De Gaulle because of the French
President's decision to give up France's colonies in North Africa (or
specifically Algeria). The conspirators see this as a betrayal of their
patriotic values. However almost as soon as we read this, we
discover that other people behind the conspiracy have not yet given
up. They are determined to punish De Gaulle for what they think of
as his treason against France and they decide to hire a foreign
professional assassin who goes by the codename of "the Jackal". By
this stage, we are already hooked.

How about another, this one from Ken Follet's *Lie Down with Lions*:

> The men who wanted to kill Ahmet Yilmaz
> were serious people.

This is perhaps even more direct than the Frederick Forsyth book.
The Day of the Jackal lulls us into a false sense of security with its
quiet opening clause referring to the weather, saving the sting-in-the-
tail for the second clause of the sentence. But the Follet book uses a
different approach. The sentence has only one clause and hits us with
action rather than mystery right from the word go. Of course, here
too we want to know certain things. Who is Ahmet Yilmaz? Who is
trying to kill him? And why? These are all mystery questions. But
there is another question that confronts us — an action question that

186

fits in with the action that we have been launched into right from the start: *will they succeed*?

The attention-grabbing beginning does not necessarily have to be in the first sentence. It can be lower down in the first paragraph. Here are two examples from my own personal experience. The first is a book called *The Temple of the Mind* that I started but never completed. It was to have been a long book written in the first person about the career of an American from his student days when he met the woman who was to become his wife, through his legal career, up to his entry into politics and the scandal that hits him when he is at the pinnacle of success. Using the begin-at-the-end technique that we will discuss in the next module, I started the book with a prologue beginning with the following:

> I have finally come to realize that a man has
> reached breaking point when he looks back
> at his childhood and thinks not how good but
> how perfect it was. Yet, as I look out of my
> penthouse window at the two federal agents
> who are coming to arrest my wife, I do not
> feel broken, merely regretful for what might
> have been.

This is an example of capturing the attention by being enigmatic. The enigma first appears in the second sentence. The first sentence, like the first clause of the opening sentence in the *Day of the Jackal*, is a quiet lead in that lulls the reader into a false sense of security. It is the second sentence that makes the reader sit forward and peer intently at the words to make sure that he has taken it in correctly. I actually saw a literary agent do this when she read that second sentence. (Sadly, she decided in the end not to represent me.)

The next example is from my second "Alex Sedaka" thriller: *No Way Out*.

> It was only a set of fingers flying across a
> keyboard. But they could work so much
> malice.

It could have been written as one long, compound sentence with two clauses. But either way, the principle is still the same. First a few words that seem pretty ordinary in themselves and then a few more words that really open up the story. The key word in the second sentence above is "malice". In creative writing, as in advertising when making a sales pitch, there are certain key words that "sell" whatever it is you're trying to sell — which in the case of a writer is your *story*. The word "malice" says to the reader: "Sit up and take notice of me!"

Up until the appearance of that red-flag word, the reader might have thought that this was just an innocent account of some one typing a letter… or even playing the piano! But once they get to the word "malice" there is no going back. This is a person with a mission, and the reader wants to know *who* is the person and *what* is the mission. Red-flag words are useful devices for grabbing the reader's attention. But they should not be used gratuitously. It is important to select the right word for the story you are writing.

The key to grabbing the reader's attention is to say something about an issue that is important and relevant to them. "Somewhere in a tropical rain forest, two iguanas were fighting," might raise a few quizzical eyebrows, and might even make the reader mildly curious, but it probably wouldn't get you very far as a writer of bestsellers. After all, how many readers care about the fate of a couple of iguanas in a tropical rain forest?

On the other hand, consider this beginning from Michael Ridpath's *Trading Reality*:

> It didn't take much to wipe twenty billion dollars off the world's bond markets. Just a small sentence. A few words transmitted simultaneously on to every screen in every dealing room around the word:
>
> 12 April. 14:46 GMT
>
> Fed Chairman Alan Greenspan warns that US interest rates are "abnormally low" and will move up shortly.

Now that's a beginning that all of us can relate to. We may not all be financial dealers or high-rolling investors. But we all live in the real world that is governed by money. Many of us have mortgages. Many of us have pension plans. Some of us have stock market investments. Even if none of these things applies to us, we still buy food and other goods. In short, we all live in the real world in which money rules, or at least talks. Also, even if few us have real fortunes, we almost all *dream* of having them. Thus, we can certainly relate to a beginning that speaks of people being buffeted by the winds of financial fortune — and *mis*fortune.

Setting the stage for the story

This is another classic technique and, to some extent, it complements the use of the opening as an attention grabber. A beginning can be used as a means of introducing the situation that forms the breeding ground for the conflict, or the background to the conflict or the place where the conflict is played out.

My first published book, *A Fool for a Client*, begins like this:

> "Your Honor," Justine Levy's voice rang out confidently, "this isn't any sort of legal gray area. Under the Sixth amendment I have the right to conduct my own defense."

Right from the opening two words we know that this is a *legal drama/thriller*. Although the words "Your Honor" could be addressed to the mayor of a town or city, they are in practice more likely to be used to address a judge. We sense that it is probably set in the United States because we associate the words "Your Honor" with American judges and "My Lord" with their British counterparts. (In fact, many judges in British courts are "Your Honor". However, in practice the words have a distinctly American connotation, if only because we have read and seen so many American courtroom dramas and thrillers.)

As we continue along the first line, we learn that it is a *woman* who is addressing the judge. This arouses our interest further. Is she a woman lawyer, fighting confidently in what is still seen by some as a

189

man's world? When we read the words "Sixth Amendment", we are given further assurance that we were right in our initial assumption that the story is set (at least partly) in *the United States*. By the time we get to the final part of the sentence about her right to conduct her own defense we know exactly what the issue is and what the story is going to be about: a female defendant conducting her own defense.

That opening sentence clearly has the effect of grabbing the reader's attention. But it also sets the stage for the entire story. We want to know what she is accused of. Is she guilty or innocent? If guilty, will she get away with it? If innocent, will she be wrongly convicted? And of course, if she is guilty, an auxiliary question arises: *why* did she do it? Does she have a valid reason? Are there any mitigating circumstances? All of these questions are encapsulated in those 29 words of the opening sentence.

In that example, although the setting is clear, the language is indirect. The book doesn't start by *literally* saying: Justine Levy is on trial for murder and she demands the right to conduct her own defense. But in practice, it amounts to that.

Sometimes the most powerful of stories can have the quietest of beginnings. Consider this opening sentence:

> Behavioral science, the FBI section that
> deals with serial murder, is on the bottom
> floor of the Academy building at Quantico,
> half-buried in the earth.

It is an extremely fact-based opening, not calculated to display any flashy pyrotechnics. Yet this is the opening sentence of Thomas Harris's *Silence of the Lambs* a thriller that was made into one of the most successful (and certainly one of the most disturbing) films of modern times. The story involves the use of behavioral science to catch a serial killer called "Buffalo Bill". In the course of the story, the heroine, a trainee FBI agent called Clarice Starling, has to consult another serial killer – the infamous Hannibal Lecter – for some insights into the mind of such a killer (Lecter is a psychiatrist in addition to being a serial killer with cannibalistic tendencies.)

Another example of using an "informational beginning" to set the stage, is the opening sentence of Ken Follet's *Eye of the Needle*:

> Early in 1944, German Intelligence was
> piecing together evidence of a huge army in
> south eastern England.

This is straightforward and routine. It starts off by telling the reader what the story is about. It could almost be the start of a synopsis for the book or the writer telling others how he came to think of the idea in the first place. But it works as well as any of the more grandiose beginnings. Simply telling the reader what the story is about is perfectly acceptable and can also be very interesting if the background subject matter is inherently interesting,

Some would say that every book has a "natural" beginning: one particular opening sentence or paragraph that is just right for the book. I wouldn't take it to quite this extreme. Some stories do cry out for a particular beginning. But others offer the writer a choice.

Suppose for example, you are planning to write a story involving an airplane that gets into difficulties because of sabotage, terrorism, personality clashes or just plain incompetence. Where might you begin the story? In the cockpit, with the plane already in flight? In the control tower of the airport? In the design lab where a young bright engineer discovers a hitherto undetected flaw in the design? In the passenger cabin? On the ground, as the passengers file innocently into the flight lounge or airplane?

Each of the above options is valid. The choice depends on what type of book you want it to be. If it is to be a techno-thriller, then a good start might be the test lab of the company that manufactured the plane. If it is to be a disaster story, it could be the control tower or cockpit. If it is to be a "collection bin" story about the dynamics of character relationship, it could start in the flight lounge before or as the passengers board the plane. If it is to be a political thriller about terrorists, it could be in the flight lounge as the terrorists board the plane, or the place where they first plan the mission. But even among these examples, nothing is obligatory. The techno-thriller version doesn't *have* to start in the test lab. The terrorist version *could* begin in the cockpit. There are no rules written in stone, only guiding *principles*.

Sidney Sheldon's *Other Side of Midnight* starts with a prologue building up to a trial of a woman and a man for murder. Then the book goes back to the events leading up to the trial. How does the author describe this build up? The answer is in a series of vignettes in which various people who have crossed the path of one of the two defendants arrive in Athens for the trial. In these vignettes, he gives hints of their attitudes towards the woman, but doesn't give away too much. He tantalizes the reader and makes us want to know more. Then we have to wait until the last section of the book for the trial itself. But on the way, we read about the events and incidents in which these spectators at the trial encountered the woman who is in the dock.

This approach doesn't just give us an introduction to the story, it also introduces the *characters*. This leads to another use of the opening of the book...

Introducing the hero or villain

Just as the opening can introduce a place, it can also be used to introduce a person. As novels are usually about people, it is quite legitimate to use the opening to introduce a major character: hero or villain. Robert Dailey's *Hands of a Stranger* shows a simple, straightforward way in which this can be done:

> The first rape victim that morning was a
> nineteen-year-old black girl. The second was
> a thirty-eight-year-old housewife. Assistant
> District Attorney Judith Adler could not do
> much for her either.

Here the author wastes no time in telling us explicitly that the story is about a female prosecutor, who as we later learns heads the sex crimes unit in Manhattan.

The character is almost certainly inspired by – if not actually based on – Linda Alice Fairstein who was also to some extent the role model for prosecutors in thrillers by several other writers too. Perhaps because of this, Ms Fairstein went on to become a successful thriller writer in her own right!

Of course, the beginning of the book can also be used to introduce the villain, as illustrated by the opening of Dev Stryker's *End Game*:

> *He. .*

> …ignored the escalator – he had never trusted them – and walked down the wide marble steps of the Port Authority Bus Terminal, pretending to be a tourist, looking around as if he had never seen the place before.

> But he was very familiar with the building, and while it was well lit and bright, especially compared to Manhattan's ancient subway stations, he was sure it was the most depressing place in America.

The chapter goes on to describe how "he" allows himself to be picked up by another man whom he then kills. This is the beginning of a killing spree that plays out over New York City like a chess game on a giant board.

Establishing the genre with the beginning

The beginning of the book can also establish the genre. This is not what the beginning is meant for, but it's one of the things the beginning can do. Take this opening:

> "I, Florentyna Kane, do solemnly swear…"

> *"I, Florentyna Kane, do solemnly swear…"*

> "… that I will faithfully execute the office of the president of the United States…"

> *"… that I will faithfully execute the office of the president of the United States…"*

There's no doubt about that book's about! The extract is from Jeffrey Archer's *Shall We Tell the President*. To some extent, the title already let's the cat out of the bag. But there is a difference between *revealing* the genre and *establishing* the genre. Obviously, the reader is going to have some idea of what the book is about before they start to read the book. But the establishing of the genre is very much like setting the stage. It effectively sets the *mood* for the story and thus complements the setting of the stage.

The beginning of my own *Fool for a Client* made it clear from the opening two words - "Your Honor" – that it was a legal thriller. This was not the primary purpose. But it was one of the effects. And it is a useful by-product. It confirms the reader's expectations and makes the reader feel at home with their choice of book. Nothing is more uncomfortable for a reader than to feel that he is reading a book in a different genre to the one he expected. I once bought a book that appeared from the blurb to be a first-person woman in jeopardy thriller. It was about a woman in jeopardy, but it was more in the form of a social commentary on the problems women face in society. It was very interesting in its own right, and I would have been quite happy to read it on another day. But on that day, I was expecting to read a suspense thriller of the woman-in-jeopardy sub-genre.

Types of beginning

There are many different types of beginning. A book can start at the beginning of the events. It can start at some event well before the main story. It can also start in the middle or towards the end of the story and then go back to the beginning of the sequence of events. Below are just a few examples.

Starting after the beginning

Starting at the beginning is a fairly conventional but perfectly legitimate way of starting a book. Of course, in some ways, it is hard to define what the beginning is. Many of the classic Agatha Christie mysteries started off with the conflict and build-up, followed by the murder, followed by the investigation. It could therefore be argued that a mystery that starts off with the murder, and then proceeds to a retroactive investigation, is not truly starting at the *beginning*. We will discuss this whole broad issue of the sequence of presentation under the heading of "Story Structures" in the next module.

However, for the purpose of beginning at the beginning, suffice it to say that if the retroactive investigation involves interviewing witnesses *after* the murder and asking them questions about events that happened *before* the murder, then to start with the murder is indeed to start at the *beginning*. If, on the other hand, the events before the murder are *dramatized* rather than narrated in dialogue by characters, then the murder is *not* the beginning. The definition of the "beginning" at the structural level of storytelling is therefore the earliest part of the sequence of events that is *dramatized*.

Starting at the end (it's risky, but it can work)

A cynic would say that starting at the end means that you think your story isn't all that interesting. The logic goes: your story wades through a lot of background detail that most readers don't want to read (but have to understand or there wouldn't be a story), so you subject them to the ending — the only interesting bit of your story — so as to grab their attention and force them to read all the boring background details. There are cases when this may in fact be true, and as a writer you should be on your guard against using the starting-at-the-end technique as a means of glossing over a boring story or a boring presentation of the background. But this does not mean that the criticism is inevitably true, or that you should always refrain from using this method.

The prologues to Sidney Sheldon's *The Other Side of Midnight* and *Stranger in the mirror* as well as my own incomplete *The Temple of the Mind* are examples of this technique in action. In these cases, the stories were spread out over a period of time rather than tightly focused and chronologically compressed. This is sometimes called a "horizontal novel" as opposed to the shorter, more time-condensed "vertical novel", although it has to be said that horizontal novels – or sagas as they are sometimes called – do not usually head so inexorably towards an intense and highly focused conclusion as books by Sidney Sheldon.

What is important here is that it is precisely for this sort of story that the use of the prologue starting at the climax is such a useful tool. This is not because the background or history is uninteresting. It is just that the background doesn't have the same compelling reader involvement as the climax. Once the reader *knows* that this is not just a saga about a promising law student, or about two women who have relationships – at different times – with the same no-goodnik, the story holds their attention. They know that these people have a *destiny*, and they are ready to read through the background to understand that destiny.

One final note here: although prologues starting after the main events in the story are becoming fashionable, the original use of a prologue was to describe events that occurred long *before* the main events of the story. This method is still valid today — especially if there *are* significant events in your story that occur a long time before the main events and that can be safely told to the reader *without* telegraphing the end or ruining the surprise.

The "quiet" beginning

There is an opening sequence of moves in the game of chess called the "Giucco Piano". This opening, although now considered bland an uninspiring, was once extremely popular and in fact could lead to some real pyrotechnics in the middle-game. I hope that non-chessplayers will excuse this apparent digression, but the reason I mention it is because the words "Giucco Piano" mean "Quiet Game". And like the Giucco Piano in chess, the quiet beginning of a book can lead to some real pyrotechnics as the story gets underway. We have seen this already with the beginnings of *The Eye of the Needle* and *The Silence of the Lambs*. Here's another example:

> The face of Nicholas Easter was slightly hidden by a display filled with slim cordless phones, and he was not looking directly at the hidden camera but somewhere off to the left, perhaps at a customer, or perhaps at a counter where a group of kids hovered over the latest electronic games from Asia.

The book is *The Runaway Jury*, by John Grisham. The beginning introduces the main character of the story as he is being watched by others. He is a prospective juror in a massive civil litigation case against the tobacco industry and he is being vetted by people working for that industry to determine if he is a suitable juror. But the opening does not immediately jump in to those details. The first line is quiet and non-committal, an the story goes on to tell us that he is being watched by some one anonymous. As the chapter continues, these details are fleshed out.

This is important because even the quietest of beginnings must supply us with *something* to lead the reader into the story, even if the opening sentence or paragraph is free of pyrotechnics. Here is an example of a quiet beginning from my second published thriller, *The Other Victim*:

> A streak of red hung over the horizon like a wound in the sky.
>
> It hovered in the wake of the setting sun's departure, as if reluctant to acknowledge the day's departure. There seemed to be no force holding it in place, no invisible strings to suspend it from above, no breath of power to prop it up from below. Yet it stayed in place, held there by an inertia so final that not even the encroaching darkness could dislodge it.
>
> It was a trivial sight. But it held Tony spellbound for a few seconds as he stepped our of Leicester Square Tube station. When the moment passed, he turned right and walked into the warm air, pausing again, to take a deep breath, against the humidity. He felt someone tugging at his sleeve, puncturing his daydream with an irritating blast of reality.
>
> 'Come on Tony!'
>
> It was Phil. Cool, unemotional Phil.

There is something symbolic and metaphoric in this description with its use of the sunset, because for one of these two, it is really a sunset finale: he is killed later in this opening chapter. But at this stage the

197

reader doesn't know that. All he knows is that these two are in London's bustling, crowded Leicester Square and it is sunset on a warm day. As the passage continues, however, we read the following:

> In time with their first few steps across the
> red brick pavement into the throngs and
> glitter of the square, two pairs of eyes
> followed them, focusing squarely on Tony...
> and two pairs of feet kept a steady distance
> between them.

This is the first hint that something heavy is going down.

The enigmatic beginning

Beginnings can also entice the reader into the story by the aura of mystery that they evoke. The following is from a book called *The Alienist*, by Caleb Carr:

> Theodore is in the ground.

Kind of spooky, no? The book is about a serial killer at the turn of the century, when such things were less well known and far less understood. A short while later we learn that the "Theodore" in question is actually Theodore Roosevelt. This sets the period, but saps the enigma of some of its power. But by then our interest is already aroused: we are hungry to know more. Or how about this, from Tom Clancy's *Games of State* from the *Op Center* series.

> Until a few days ago, twenty-one-year-old
> Jody Thompson didn't have a war.

Want to know who Jody Thompson is? And what kind of war is it that Jody Thompson now has? I certainly do.

Elements of the beginning

When thinking about the opening, remember that it is characterized by various parts. These are the opening sentence, the opening paragraph, the opening page and the opening chapter. Each of these requires a certain amount of thought.

The opening sentence

This is perhaps the hardest element of the lot. That is why we have
devoted so much attention to it already. You will have to decide
when, where and with whom among your cast of characters to begin
the book, before you can write the opening sentence. But even when
you have made those decisions, the first sentence is – frankly – a
bitch.

If the opening sentence is designed to grab the reader's attention, it
can have *mystery* (like the first sentence of Frederick Forsyth's *The
Day of the Jackal*), *impact* relating to people's lives (like the opening
to Michael Ridpath's *Trading Reality*) or *violence*. A book called
Tony Rome by Marvin H Albert (later made into a film with Frank
Sinatra) began with the narrator – Tony Rome – himself, telling the
reader that he opened the door of his office to find some one he
knew lying there dead with a bullet hole in the middle of his
forehead. It's crude, but it's effective!

The opening paragraph

The opening paragraph must serve the same purpose as the opening
sentence. If the opening sentence is the "handle", then the opening
paragraph is the pot. The aim is to hold the pot under the nose of the
reader and tempt him to eat the meal by the appetizing smell of the
food. You do not have to grab the reader's attention with the opening
sentence – although it is obviously good if you do – but by the end
of the opening paragraph, your readers should feel that they are onto
something good.

In general it is better to decide what you want to say in the opening
paragraph as a whole – or even the opening page – and then go back
and decide on what to put into the opening sentence. The reason for
this is that while it may be good to play for effect, in the opening
sentence, the reader isn't interested in effect: he or she is interested in
the story. Therefore, you must first decide when and where your
story is going to begin. This in turn dictates the opening sentence
and paragraph.

There are a number of things that an opening paragraph might do in relation to the opening sentence. It may explain and expand upon an enigmatic opening sentence. It may give more details about a character who has just been introduced in the opening sentence. It may *step back* from the opening sentence and lead the reader away from it.

In general is advisable to make the opening paragraph short. If you must put in a lot of information that naturally belongs together in a single paragraph, it is much better to find a way to put it into the *second* paragraph and keep the first paragraph short. Readers can be frightened off by a long first paragraph. Also, once the reader has got past the first paragraph, they have a sense of having taken the first step on the reader's journey and are more likely to continue.

The first page

The first page should already begin to move the story forward. This doesn't mean that it has to *tell* a story. But it does mean that it has to give the reader the feeling that he has moved off the starting line. To illustrate this point, let's take a made up beginning.

> It was quiet when he entered the room. There was a certain eerie silence that pervaded the atmosphere: a sense of something that shouldn't have been there... yet was. It was no exactly the silence, nor yet the stillness... but something. He sensed it and struggled to understand it, his ears straining against the silence to detect the faintest trace of sound.
>
> If there had been the faintest whisper in any corner of the room, or even beyond the walls, he would have heard it. But he heard nothing. Not even the ghosts of the past. If there had been any sounds in this room, they neither reverberated off the walls nor resonated off the furniture.
>
> And it was not just the silence that struck him. It was also the stillness, the frightening terrifying stillness. It was the sort of stillness you'd expect to see if some one had pressed

the freeze frame on a video. Except that in this case there wasn't even that trace of flickering to tell you that the process is alive. This was the stillness of death. Only the rhythmic beating of his own heart told him that there was life in the room.

He stood still, realizing that movement was pointless. There was no resistance to move against, no danger to run from. After the initial apprehension of the unknown, he felt nothing. It was as if he stepped into oblivion and now there was no need to act. In the stillness and silence the need for any form of action evaporated. He was free to merge with the stillness… free to live in the silence. As it enveloped him, he pondered his next move.

In some ways, the passage is quite atmospheric and enigmatic – even mystifying. But it also has a number of things that are plainly wrong with it – at least if it were used as the opening of a book. The main flaw is that it doesn't take the reader *anywhere*. It evokes the stillness and silence, but it does nothing else. If this were a mood piece, it might almost be a meritorious piece of writing. It might even work in the *middle* of a thriller, once we know a bit about the character in question. But as a *beginning* to a thriller it is somewhat static.

That is not to say that it doesn't *start off* well. The enigmatic opening sentence is fine. It certainly grabs the reader's attention. Even the whole of the first paragraph builds upon the. But by the second paragraph we, as reader's want to know more. And we are not getting it. Who is this man? What is this room? Where is this room? Why is it silent? What time of day is it? What *should* be happening in the room or beyond that makes the silence so unnatural? Has some disaster happened like a nuclear explosion, and this is the silence of the aftermath? His he arrived at the wrong time? Are his friends lying in wait, having planned a surprise party for him? We just don't know. And the author is not telling us

Now you might think: *surely this is good. The beginning has caused us to ask questions. Isn't the beginning supposed to do that? Isn't that what gets us to read on?*

The answer is that all of this is true if we were talking about the first *paragraph*. But by the time we get to the end of the first page, at least *some* of the questions should have been answered. And yet, in the example above, not only have none of the questions been answered, but the same questions have been *asked several times*. There is very little in the second, third and fourth paragraphs that is not simply a restatement of what has already appeared in the first. In effect, those paragraphs are just spinning things out, almost like a delaying tactic.

By all means, write atmospheric beginnings. But make sure that as you move on from the first paragraph, the story moves on from atmosphere to action, or at least to background information.

The first chapter

The role of the first chapter is much harder to define, as chapters themselves can vary greatly in length. How you divide your book into chapters is a subject in itself. You might write short chapters, with each chapter functioning as a separate scene. On the other hand, you might write long chapters, broken into separate scenes by line breaks.

How then do you decide what to put into the first chapter? If the chapter is to be a one-scene chapter then you simply take the starting point that you selected for your story (relevant incident, character or place) and write it up until the scene comes to a logical conclusion. If on the other hand the chapter is a multi-scene chapter, then it should be guided by two principles. The first is that it should have the same general balance as the other multi-scene chapters. The second is that it should end at a point that leaves the reader hungry for more — as indeed should all the chapters, with the (possible) exception of the last.

What do I mean by "the same general balance as the other multi-scene chapters"? Well let's say that your story is about three principle characters and that the chapters generally have at least one scene with each of these: then your first chapter should also have at least one scene with each character. Or, let's say that the story alternates between past and present and most chapters have one scene from the past and one from the present. Then, barring some compelling reason to the contrary, the first chapter should be just like this. Or finally, suppose the story is set over several days and each chapter contains the events of that day. The first chapter (unless it is a prologue set at a different time to the main body of the story) should narrate the events of the first day.

Ending the first chapter at a point that leaves the reader hungry for more is important for obvious reasons. This can be when a murder is committed, when a body is found, when a lawyer gets a phone call, when a suspect is arrested, when the widget is stolen, when the hero is attacked out of the blue, when a relationship breaks up or any of a dozen other cliff-hanging chapter endings.

Chapter 10 – Okay... but how do I *end* my novel?

Types of ending

Just as the opening chapter must end at an exciting point, the book must end at a satisfying one. The ending of a thriller can contain a revelation, a sting-in-the-tail, leave the reader in a particular state of mind or can simply tie up the loose end.

The revelation

The most obvious choice of ending is one that reveals the truth. In a thriller we know that *some one* did something but we are waiting to find out who or what or why or even simply will they succeed. In a romance we want to know if the got it together or more generally who ends up with whom. In science fiction we want to know the result. In some cases, the result might be a prelude to a sequel.

But even in thrillers, on can drill down into greater detail. In a whodunit the revelation means who did it. A police procedural might end in an arrest or the fatal shooting of a suspect as he resists.. In a legal thriller, the revelation might be the verdict or the aftermath to the verdict.

The sting-in-the-tail

Closely related to the revelation is the sting-in-the-tail, a feature most commonly associated with the writings of Guy de Maupassant and O. Henry. Very often a sting-in-the-tail *is* a revelation. But not all revelations constitute a sting-in -the tail. After all, in a classic whodunit, for example, the readers know that *some one* did it. They just don't know who.

A real sting-in-the-tail occurs when the reader isn't expecting anything. For example if it turns out that the victim isn't dead after all, *that* is a sting-in-the-tail. If after the murderer has *apparently* been revealed, it turns out that the murderer was some one else, *that* is a sting-in-the-tail. If it turns out that the detective who is investigating is actually the guilty party, *that* is a sting-in-the-tail. Or if it turns out that some one tried to kill the victim and thinks they succeeded but we find out at the last minute that another cause of death intervened – *that* is a sting-in-the-tail. Or if the murderer ends up getting killed unexpectedly when it looks like he is merely going to be arrested and sent to trial (or appears to have escaped).

But the main feature of the sting-in-the-tail is that it occurs at the *very* end, when the reader thinks all the surprises are over.

The tying-up of loose ends

This is also related to the Revelation ending, standing on the other side to the sting-in-the-tail. If the sting-in-the-tail is the revelation-*plus*, the tying up of loose ends is the revelation-minus – the housekeeping that has to be done to leave the stage clean and tidy.

In a complex story, after the big surprise has been presented, there will still almost certainly be many details that need explaining. These loose ends cannot usually be tied up before the surprise ending because that would probably telegraph the ending. So instead, they must be tied up *after*. That process would, in such a case, constitute the ending of the book.

You should not think of this type of ending as an anti-climax. In the first place, the reader will certainly want to know these details. So you will be giving the readers what they want. Secondly, if your hero is to be used again in a series of books then this will keep your readers' attention focused on the hero rather than the villain. Of course, if you *can* tie up the loose ends first and *then* hit the reader with a sting-in-the-tail so much the better.

In m thriller *The Other Victim*, the entire last chapter is devoted to tying up the loose ends after the guilty parties have been identified and dealt with. It would have been nice to end with the big twist that comes at the end of the penultimate chapter. But this would simply not have been practical. One often finds this in classic thrillers too.

After the murderer has been revealed and caught, the detective explains to his sidekick a few pieces of supplementary information that clarify the missing details.

Leaving the reader in a particular state of mind

The ending can also serve another purpose and that is to help the readers wind down their emotions or alternatively to raise their level of excitement and leave them feeling as if they've been kicked in the ribs (this is the feeling they should get if they have just been subjected to a good sting-in-the-tail). If the aim of the ending is to help the reader wind down, the writer will want to leave the reader satisfied, relieved, or relaxed.

The Other Victim had a final chapter in which the lawyer hero and policewoman heroine are on holiday together in Eilat, Israel and the hero is answering the heroine's questions about the case. You might think that it is surprising that by this stage the policewoman still doesn't know all the answers. The answer is that she *does* know the basic facts, but what the hero is telling her is *how* he latched on to them. What is really happening of course is that the *author* (i.e. yours truly) is telling the *reader* about all the clues they missed. It is the author's way of showing that he has been fair and given the reader a sporting chance to guess the surprises ahead of time.

But the reason that I set this last chapter in the context of a relaxing holiday in the sunshine was because in addition to tying up the loose ends, I wanted to assure the reader that the hero and heroine end up together. I also wanted to wind drown the readers' emotions and leave them in a calm and tranquil state. This is not always my aim when I end a book. My third thriller *Tarnished Heroes* ended on a note that was calculated to leave the reader in a state of emotional turbulence, agonizing over the ethics of the hero and the morality of the ending. Here is how it read.

> She knew that what he was doing took
> courage □ more courage than confronting the
> killer or telling the truth at the inquest – but
> as with those other courageous actions, it
> was something that Neil had to do alone. She

would always be close at hand to give him moral support. But just as he had faced the darkness alone, he would also have to face the light of day alone – even if he didn't like what he saw.

It is important not to place too much emphasis on trying to manipulate the reader's emotions. Leaving the reader in a given state of mind should *complement* the final revelation, surprise or tying up of the loose ends. It should never supplant them.

The ending can also leave the reader angry, amazed, confused or hungry for more. In a didactic novel, the ending can also leave the reader concerned or angry. For example, if you wanted to make a statement against the death penalty, you could write a book set in country (and time) where they have the death penalty and then have an innocent man convicted and executed. However, be aware of the fact that unhappy endings tend to turn off the reader, making them less likely to recommend the book to others. Alternatively you could write an ambiguous book in which the guilt or innocence is uncertain.

In other genres too – like romance – you can use the ending to steer the reader's emotional state to the point where you want it to be.

The last page

By the final page, you should be preparing to wrap up your story. Of course, it is possible to save up one final twist for the last page, or even the last line – especially if you are planning a sting-in-the-tail ending. But in general, the surprises are quite likely to be over by now and you will be in the loose ends or winding-down phase of the story.

There is no hard and fast rule for the last page of the last few paragraphs. You may be trying to convey to the reader how the principle characters will continue their lives now that the story is over. For example, you might end a story in which a husband and wife have been through trials and tribulations together, with the woman telling her husband that she is pregnant. This could of course be a sting-in-the-tail throwaway line. But then again, he could also react to it and you could use this to show the status of the couple's relationship. One version of Nelson de Mille's *Word of Honour* ended like this. I say "one version" because while the paperback version that I read, had such an ending, it was missing from a hardback copy that I got my hands on later.

The last few paragraphs might also be used to tie up the last of the loose ends. Or they may be used to build up innocently towards a sting-in-tail. Then again, it could simply be a solemn passage about the events of the story or the place where the story took place. If the hero is a recurring character, they could even introduce the next book. I vaguely remember one of Erle Stanley Gardener's Perry Mason thrillers ending with Mason's secretary, Della Street telling the lawyer that the client sitting in the waiting room was a young female with a rather sulky look on her face. His next thriller took up on this theme under the title *The Case of the Sulky Girl.*

The final paragraph

The final paragraph has still more limited scope and can only perform one of the functions of an ending. Here's an example of an ending that is heading for a winding down of intensity.

> The following day the body of a man was buried in an unmarked grave at Père Lachaise cemetery in Paris. The death certificate showed the body to be that of an unnamed foreign tourist, killed on Sunday August 25, 1963 in a hit and run accident on the motorway outside the city. Present were a priest, a policeman, a registrar and two gravediggers. Nobody present showed any interest as the plain coffin was lowered into the ground, except the single other person who attended. When it was all over he turned round, declined to give his name and walked back down the cemetery path, a solitary figure, to return home to his wife and children.
>
> The day of the Jackal was over.

If more humorous endings are to your taste, how about this one from Clifford Irving's *Trial*. The hero lawyer has nailed the villains and is now with the new woman in his life. But he is still under stress. To relieve the tension she tells him a joke. First she asks him why they use lawyers instead of white rats in laboratory experiments. When he confesses his ignorance, she answers her own question.

> "Because there are more lawyers than white
> rats. Lawyers clean up their messes faster
> than white rats do. If you have any sense,
> you don't get personally attached to lawyers.
> But mostly," she added with a smile he
> would treasure, "because there are some
> things white rats just won't do."

The closing sentence

Closing sentences are often designed for impact, like opening sentences. Except that in the case of a *closing* sentence, it is more likely to be *quiet* impact. Forsyth's "The day of the Jackal was over," is an example of this, as is my own ending to *Tarnished Heroes*.

Stan Lee's *Dunn's Conundrum* ends with the hero together with his new girlfriend who happens to be the girlfriend of his former colleague. Now, however, his former colleague is his enemy. The hero knows that he is still under observation by secret cameras and he decides to taunt his enemy. First he undresses the young lady before the "hidden" cameras and then comes the final line:

> "Let's leave the lights on," he said.

A more sedate ending is to be found in Ken Follet's *The Eye of the Needle*, a story about the second Word War told in flashback.

> Until David jumped off his grandfather's lap
> and knocked the cup of tea to the floor and
> the spell was broken.

A good example of quiet ending is this, from Ted Allbeury's *Snowball*. The hero is in bed recuperating after a gruelling assignment. The final paragraph describes a vase by his bedside with

209

the red roses, their drooped heads and fallen petals. Then comes the haunting quiet sentence:

> They were nearly dead but not quite.

Literally, it's about the roses. But symbolically it's about the hero; and not even about his body —about his spirit, after all he has been through.

Another, less symbolic final sentence is to be found in John Creasey's *A Splinter of Glass* – a book about a gold bullion robbery.

> When at last he rang off, he felt very contented.

Having said all this, it is not as difficult to write a good ending as it sounds. If the book as a whole is good, you will find that the ending comes to you quite naturally.

Chapter 11 – How to work *professionally* as a writer

Okay, so you've got your plot and you have a rough idea of how you want to tell it in terms of progression of events, flashbacks, etc. But how do you organize the model structure into a precise series of chapters, scenes events, etc? We have learned about characterization, but how do you maintain consistency in your characters? We have learned about description, but how do you maintain consistency in your descriptions of places?

Planning

Books can be planned in detail or you can work from a very rough and vague idea. The same is true for character details. There is no hard and fast rule. But let's look at some of the ways you can work.

Card index for plot events

A good way of handling multi-plot novels or for organizing the strands of a story together is to use a card index (or the computerized equivalent) for individual plot events. If your story consists of two parallel stories, or a present story interspersed with flashbacks you can dovetail these cards together. Alternatively you can use post-it notes (again there is a software equivalent). You can also simply type it into a file in bold or using a colored background and then flesh out the details as you write the book – deleting the "notes" along the way. And if the story has multiple strands, you could make several columns or a grid or table. You could even use a spreadsheet.

The first stage is to write out all the major elements of the storylines, one event per card. The advantage of working this way is that you do not have to think up the events in any particular order. Most stories are developed over a period of time, anything from a few days to a few years. You can write down the most important events first and then add further events afterwards as they occur to you. You can do this for each of the story strands.

Suppose, for example, your story consists of parallel strands in which a married man has gone missing but the police think has simply left home of his own free will, while at the same time another man's body has turned up in an apparently unrelated episode which turns out to be linked. In the missing husband story, the wife might call in a private detective to look for her missing husband. In the other story the police would be investigating the murderer. You might make notes like: "wife finds husband's clothes and suitcase gone" on one card, "detective finds out from colleague about husband's affair with secretary who left two weeks earlier after embezzling company money" on another card, etc. At the same time, you would also be making notes about the dead person and the investigation like: "pathologist tells police that cause of death was blow to head from blunt object", "police find large sum of cash in dead man's home."

By now you have probably sensed where this story is going. Once you have your details in place you take the cards for each of the storylines and arrange them in internal chronological order. Then you can intersperse them in whichever way suits you. The reason I recommend doing things this way is because although it is possible to jump around in time randomly, if you have a flashback story, it is best to present it in an internally chronologically order.

For example if your story is about some one who commits a revenge murder with elaborate planning and is then on trial for it, you could intersperse an orderly chronological account of the preparation and murder with an orderly and chronological presentation of the trial. But to make it a surprise you could save up the motive for the end. Or you could describe the preparation and murder anonymously, without revealing who is doing it, thus leaving the reader to wonder if the person on trial is the right person. Maybe the murderer not only set out to kill one person but also to frame another!

You may have to play around as you intersperse the cards (or their software equivalent) because you may not want to reveal one particular detail or event in one story strand before revealing another event in another strand. You may also find that you have to create additional events, not as padding but to separate events that you do not want to occur together. For example, if two events combine to create a clue, you might want to separate them with an innocuous event or scene so as not to make the clue too obvious.

Card index for characters

This is also a useful way of keeping your details in order and maintaining consistency, especially if you're planning a series of books with recurring characters. On your cards you can write physical details, like height, weight, hair color eye color, etc. You can write what type of clothes the repeat characters wear. You can add their taste in food and drink. Most importantly you can put their backgrounds. I say "most importantly" because you will almost certainly want to reveal their backgrounds over a series of books.

If the hero is ex-military, for example, you may wish to have him reminisce (whether by stream of consciousness or dialogue) about his past. But you will not put his entire career into one book. Rather he will remember or speak about particular episodes at particular times in particular stories, ideally in a way that relates to the events of that particular story.

Also of course you can add additional key information to the cards as the hero's adventures add to his life history. Also of course, you can add further cards about his family and the various people who come into his life.

When planning or writing subsequent books, you can consult these cards to get the details right before you commit yourself to writing something that may wreck the consistency of your characters.

You do not of course have to use physical index cards as your medium. You can take advantage of the power of modern technology to create index cards on a computer. This is also useful for handling the plot details, as the cards can be re-arranged electronically. If you want something more sophisticated you can add your fictional characters to a contact manager or even create a full-blown database for your characters.

213

Index cards can also serve an auxiliary purpose; by laying them side by side you can avoid making your characters too much like one another. If you notice recurring characteristics that are non-essential, you might want to change some of these characteristics to promote variety and differentiation among your characters.

Meticulous planning

Some writers, like Sinclair Lewis and Irving Wallace, used to create elaborate diagrams and floor-plans of rooms and streets where their stories were set. They did this so that when they described people entering or exiting or picking up objects there would be a kind of cinematic continuity to these events. It also freed their minds to concentrate on literary details, safe in the knowledge that the technical details were already taken care of and that consistency could be assured by a mere side-glance at a chart or diagram.

I personally have never used this method, but it is a perfectly good method to use. If the geography or layout of a place is important to a story, it may well be desirable or even necessary to use such a device. However, it is important to use the information from such diagrams sparingly. The aim of drawing such diagrams is not to give the reader a complete textual description of every wall, door and window, but rather to guide the writer when he narrates *action* set against the backdrop of the scenery.

Testing your dialogue

One of the problems you may sometimes encounter when writing dialogue is making it sound realistic to the ear. Dialogue that seemed so clever when you wrote it the first time, often doesn't sound quite so good when you read it back. Worse still, you may not realize that your dialogue is bad until some one points it out to you. And of course if you are going the conventional route of seeking print publishing by a reputable publisher (as distinct from a "subsidy publisher"), the person who points it out is the publisher, they might just point it out *in a rejection letter*, which is rather late in the day to do anything about it — at least as far as *that* publisher is concerned.

214

One way to solve this problem is to read the dialogue out aloud, either on your own or with a friend. The latter calls for more courage, but it will also be more effective. If you can read the dialogue to a friend, without blushing, that is a sign that it is probably good dialogue. Better still, if your *friend* can read the dialogue without laughing or avoiding your eyes, it is almost certainly good dialogue!

Research

There are endless debates about research. Some say that unless you are writing about something you know from personal experience research is a must. Others say that it is an excuse for delaying writing. I have often found that I spend a great deal of time doing research for a book that never gets written. This can be because I change my mind, because I cannibalized the book for several others, because I lose my enthusiasm for the storyline or because I only conceived the idea in the first place for a publisher who, in the end, didn't like it. However, research that I do for one book almost invariably finds it's way into another so the research is never really wasted.

When writing from enthusiasm rather than experience, the amount of research you need to do depends to a large extent on how accurate you want your book to be. I say "accurate" rather than "realistic" because there is a difference between what *seems* realistic to the average reader and the way things actually work in specialist fields like criminal investigation, law or military matters. Most of your readers will not know any more about these things than you do. If you are as knowledgeable as the average reader, you will be able to make your book *realistic* to those readers without doing any research at all. But it will not necessarily be *accurate*.

If you are aiming for accuracy, you must do research. But what sort of research?

Let's say you're writing a thriller about a police investigation. You will want to know how the police go about investigating a crime. In the old days, you might find a friendly policeman and ask him. Now we live in the age of the internet and powerful search engines. These days it is possible to find the radio codes used by various police forces, the assignment of courtrooms in many cities, the bail schedule for different categories of crime in many counties. I have used this method when researching courtroom dramas and thrillers set in the USA, even though I am British. I also used Google Earth and Street View to plan car chases!

I also hooked up – via some internet forum – with a woman who actually worked in courtroom security in the very courtroom in Oakland where a rape trial in my second Alex Sedaka thriller (*No Way Out*) was set.

You can also log on to websites dealing with various aspects of forensic science, including academic websites, which might give you access to specialist articles. I logged onto a site run by the FBI (I think) that explained about DNA and its uses, including testing procedures, standards, different types of DNA etc. I have to admit that I did rather tend to *overuse* this research, making the thriller unnecessarily complicated.

But in any case, bear in mind that although the printed or electronic word are useful sources of information, *they cannot beat experience!* To get the feel of a police investigation, it is always better to talk with a policeman than to read a text book, whether online or in print. The same goes for a lawyer, a politician or anyone else.

Of course this is easier said than done. For example, when I was writing my third book, *Tarnished Heroes*, I needed to write a chase scene set in the tunnels of London Underground, in which the killer is being pursued by a maverick policeman who has gone off on his own in breach of orders. So how did I do it? I wrote to the management of the Northern Line (one of the lines on the London Underground), telling them who I was and what I was writing and asking if I could see the control room in action, visit a station that was partly built but never opened, ride in the tunnel-cleaning train and walk a section of track with one of their track-checking staff when the power was switched off at night.

They couldn't let me ride the tunnel-cleaning train because of very strict operating regulations, but I got all the other things I requested. They showed me the control room and I spoke to several of the staff in the late evening when they were running the last trains and closed down the system (just the period that my story covered). I visited the "Old Bull and Bush", a station that had been excavated at tunnel level but never completed or opened. And I got to walk a section of track from Camden Town to Golders Green, speaking into a mini-cassette recorder – which tells you how long ago this was! This research experience gave me not just the factual knowledge but the *feeling* of loneliness in the tunnels and the sights, sounds and smells of that environment.

Now my point is this: it's nice to do research, but if I hadn't already had two published thrillers under my belt by a reputable publisher I would probably have never been able to do this research. First of all, I am a naturally shy person and if I hadn't got a track record to use as my calling card, I wouldn't have had the moxie to make the request in the first place. Even if I had, it is quite likely that they would have refused, or at best fobbed off with a half-hour conversation with a station manager.

Instead I spoke to a duty manager and several other experienced operational staff, in addition to seeing places which ordinary members of the public do not get to see. In fairness, it has to be said that having me there also gave them something of value: it broke the monotony of another dull nightshift of work. So it is possible that they might have granted my requests even if I had presented myself to them as a budding author rather than a published one.

When researching that same book, I also got to see the workings of a radio station in action, which was vitally important for the story, as the heroine is a tough (even bitchy) presented of a radio phone-in program. Again, I don't know whether they would have invited me up to the station if I had not got a track record to show them.

One of the important things to remember about research is that you should resist the temptation to show the reader how much you know. Even if you are writing an "information novel", you should remember that it is the *story* that your reader is interested in, not your scholarship. There is always a great temptation to try and put in as much of the research as you can cram in, by having one of the characters tell another about how this or that system operates — or even telling the reader directly. But this is a mistake. You should tell your readers enough to ensure that they know what is going on, but no more than that.

Even very good and highly successful writers sometimes get carried away with the desire to show how much research they have done. Frederick Forsyth, in *The Odessa File*, has the hero being trained to infiltrate ODESSA (the organization of former SS officers). In the process, he is taught about the structure of the SS. This is very interesting, but even if we had simply heard the start of the Chapter and then been *told* that the lecture went on with each section of the SS being carefully explained, it would still have been effective. We didn't really need to hear all the details that the chapter went into.

I am not criticizing Forsyth's decision to include these details. The details he provided did have the secondary effect of impressing upon the reader the scale and size and power of the SS. But this example does show how hard it is to get the balance right.

A further purpose of research is to make sure that you do not make outright silly mistakes. However the flip side of this is that if you *do* need to take literary license to make your story work, you should feel free to do so – within limits – even if it offends the purists. I did this in my first book and was never challenged on it.

Self-motivation

One of the problems that writer's often face is that of motivating themselves to write. One suggestion often heard is set yourself a deadline, as if you are writing under contract. But this well-intentioned advice is of limited value. Even writer's who *are* under contract – and I speak from personal experience – can at times find it hard to motivate themselves to write. So how do we go about it.

Work plan − in theory and practice

The first thing to do when approaching a writing task is to set oneself a work plan with targets. This means, you work out how long the book is going to be, how long the chapters are going to be and when you want to finish it by. You then work out how many words or pages you are going to write per day or per week. If you work at a full time job, you may write very little during the week and more at the weekend. You might not even write during the week at all. Alternatively, if you are a homemaker or a part-time worker, but with children, you might work a couple of hours during weekdays and not at all at the weekend. This availability of time (and the amount of energy you have after discharging your other obligations) will affect how much writing you do.

Inevitably you will fall short of your target. The trick is not to fall *too far* short − not to let it slip too much.

Writer's block

Okay, you might say, but how *do* I motivate myself when I've got writer's block?

First of all, I have gone on record as saying that there is no such things as "writer's block, it is just a euphemism for laziness. But this is perhaps an oversimplification. Writing is not by any means the most tiring of human activity, and even typing is not really all that much of a strain.

Writer's block is generally thought of as referring to a situation in which a writer doesn't know what to say. But if a writer really has nothing to say, then he shouldn't call himself a writer. What is really happening when one has writer's block is not that the writer has nothing to say, but that he is not sure *how to say it*. Let us say for example that in the next chapter or scene of a book, the hero finds the missing handkerchief that is supposed to advance the story. In his synopsis, the author might have some brief note like "he finds the handkerchief behind the armchair". But when the writer sits down at the computer all he or she can think of to write is: "he decided to take a last ditch look behind the armchair, and lo and behold, the handkerchief was there!"

Duh! That's not much is it! This line is supposed to be the cue for a short chapter, or a few pages of a long chapter. Yet all the author can manage is one compound sentence! At this point the writer panics. He knows that if this is all he writes of the event, then he is just re-writing the outline. Of course he knows that he is *not* supposed to deliberately *pad* his thriller with meaningless verbiage! But he needs more than just: "he looked behind armchair and found the handkerchief." In other words he knows what he has to say, but the only way he can think of saying it is in a straightforward, perfunctory manner that takes no time at all, is too sudden and leaves the reader with no suspense or sense of progress.

The writer knows what has to happen next – that's why writer's write a synopsis first – but he doesn't know how to go about saying it. Anything he writes will come up considerably short. So he feels depressed. The feeling of not knowing *how* to say what he wants to say manifests itself as "I don't know *what* to say," – in other words, "I've got writer's block."

The remedy to writer's block – and it is easier said than done – is basically two write. Even if all you can write is one or two sentences, write it anyway! Okay, you ask, but what do you do then? The answer, is see if you can stretch it into *three or four sentences*. Maybe there's another thought that you had, but didn't express. Or maybe you inserted the thought into a large unwieldy compound sentence and now you realize that the sentence can be split into two.

For example, maybe you wrote: "He looked behind the sofa, because he suddenly remembered that he hadn't looked there before, and lo and behold, he found it." Now you think that perhaps that sentence could be split into two.

> He remembered that there was one place he hadn't looked — behind the sofa. Quick as a flash he leapt to his feet and looked there, and sure enough, it was there.

Okay, you might think, that's an improvement but it's till too short. So you think about it some more and maybe you come up with the following:

> He tried to think about where the handkerchief could be. He had looked everywhere, or had he? At the back of his mind was the nagging thought that there were one or two places he hadn't looked. But where? Then it hit him! The sofa! *He hadn't looked behind the sofa.* Quick to remedy this slovenly error, he got up and moved round to the side of the sofa. Gripped with excitement, he put both hands on the arm of the sofa and moved it a few inches.
>
> Then he saw it, lying there against the skirting board.

Okay that's a bit better. But it's still hardly a chapter's worth. So you think about it more and pad it out further.

Pad it? But surely that's one thing that writers are supposed *not* to do. Isn't the golden rule write as much as you need to in order to make your point, but no more? Well yes, that is the golden rule. But when you pad it, the idea is not that this will be the final draft. Rather this is what you do in order to get the creative juices flowing. Bear in mind that the writer's block really means not that you don't know what to write, but rather that you feel that *whatever you do write will not be good.* Either you will write too little, or if you stretch it out it will just be a lot of talking gibberish that isn't really worth reading.

That may well be, but it's the talking gibberish that keeps you going when you think you're in danger of running out of ideas. It is the talking gibberish that forces you to think about what you are *trying* to say. It is the talking gibberish that makes sure that you are at your computer when you do think of a gem of a sentence or paragraph in the midst of all that talking gibberish!

As you waffle and talk gibberish, you will be thinking about the passage you are writing and somewhere along the line there is a prospect that your thoughts will lead to you suddenly thinking of a better way of saying part of what you are saying. So you might go back and rewrite that last sentence or two and realize that what you have said is not so bad. Or you might find that suddenly your talking gibberish has taken a turn for the better and so that even if the beginning of the passage is bad the end of the passage is good.

Even if you don't manage to improve the quality of your writing at this writing session, you will have something better to work with at the *next* session than a mere blank page. And that in itself is good – as it will make it easier for you to motivate yourself the next time. You may well find that what you have written is not all *complete* garbage, but rather some moderately good writing that needs some touching up and improvement here and there.

You might find that instead of rewriting the entire passage, all you have to do is split a few sentences, change a few words and phrases, insert a few phrases and sentences and make a few deletions. This may sound awfully complex, but you will probably find it a lot less daunting, psychologically, than filling a blank page. So if you force yourself to write, even when you feel you have nothing to say, this will break the scourge of writer's block. At best you will end up writing a good passage of text. At worst you will write a passage of *bad* text that you will turn into a passage of *good* text at the next session!

Chapter 12 – How do I publish and promote my book?

After you have written your book and made sure it has been properly edited and proofread, the time has come to have it published.

As this book is about self-publishing, publication is guaranteed. The question is what you make of it. First of all, I advise *against* vanity publishers - as I said very clearly in the introduction to this book. I also advised against self-publishing with a traditional printing house, because of the high up-front costs and the possibility that the book might only sell in small quantities.

But you still have several options. If you want to print your book in ink on paper, Amazon's CreateSpace offers you the ability to do it via Print-on-Demand with *no* up-front costs. They also take care of distribution and selling both through Amazon and any other channels that you designate and authorize. This might appear to put *them* in the driver's seat, *but they make no money unless the book sells!* Also you can buy copies at a reduced rate and resell them yourself.

Lulu offers a self-publication facilities, including single copies. But they leave the selling in your hands. And if you print up a batch, you are stuck with the same problem of the up-front costs and the possibility that your book might only sell in small quantities. Whilst we all hope that it will sell well, there are no guarantees. And there's an old saying about not counting your chickens before they're hatched.

So let's say that your first port of call for selling your book is Amazon's KDP (Kindle Direct Publishing) – as it should be. Assuming you have already opened a KDP account, you would go into your account, click on " Create new title" and this will take you to the screen where you enter the details of your book.

The Product Page

This is where the book is listed on Amazon. The details that you enter on your product entry page will affect how the book appears on its product page on Amazon sites (both .com and .co.{country code}.

Certain aspects are not covered below, such as ISBN, edition number, language, etc. These should be fairly straightforward and are explained in the KDP site if you click on "What's this?"

Below, I discuss those fields where some careful forethought is needed.

The Title

Obviously the title should be chosen to make an impact. But this doesn't mean you should go over the top in trying to shock your audience. The title should relate to the book. It can be powerful, haunting, mysterious, soothing, thought-provoking. But it should have some connection with what the book is about.

A glance at current Kindle bestsellers today (a Friday) includes *The Short Drop* by Matthew FitzSimmons, *Pretend You're Mine* by Lucy Score, *Rogue Lawyer* by John Grisham, *Mechanic* by Alexa Riley, *The Crossing* by Michael Connelly and *The Bad Boy Arrangement* by Nora Flite. You can look at the bestsellers on any day to get a sense of how authors title their books.

The title is not the final selling point, but it is the first. Imagine seeing the following two titles side by side: *The Village* or *Village of the Damned*. Which of the two would you pick up first?

Got it?

Subtitle, edition number, publisher

These are all self-explanatory. With regard to publisher, you can set up your own publishing company, whether by incorporating a company or simply adopting a trading name.

Author name ("Add contributors")

This should be a no-brainer, but even here there are things to think about. Do you want to write under your own name or a pen-name? If you are going to be writing books in more than one genre, do you want to write them all under the same name or use different names for different genres. On the one hand, if *one* of your books becomes a bestseller, then having all your books under the same name will help to sell the rest. On the other hand, people come to associate author names with the genre of the first book they read under that author name. If some one reads that great science fiction book you wrote under your name (or a pen-name) and then they buy another book by the same named author that turns out to be an historical thriller, the chances are they will be deeply disappointed, no matter how well-written the book. The reason for this is that people approach books with expectations. If they expect science fiction and get an Elizabethan mystery, they will be mightily disappointed.

My approach has always been to use different names for different genres – even sub-genres. Thus I write legal thrillers and police thrillers under the name David Kessler, historical/conspiracy thrillers under the name Adam Palmer, Children's/YA thrillers under the name Dan Ryan, sci-fi under the name D-PAK and chick-lit under the name Karen Dee. Some sell better than others, but I never confuse my audience.

I don't mind the public knowing – as long as they know that different author names appear on the different genres. If they want to read more than one of my genres, I am quite happy for them to do so. But I don't want to mislead them, because then they will pay me back with bad reviews.

Description

This is where you describe what your book is about. I used to believe that short descriptions are best – like the blurb that you actually see on the back cover of a paperback or on the inside flap of a hardback book. However I have since learned that the Amazon algorithm – and the Google algorithm too – is more likely to pick it up if the description is longer. One person who has written on the subject suggested that the description should be at least 500 words long and could be as much as 800. I cannot vouch for this, but it is worth noting that Amazon provides a space of 4000 *characters* for the book description, both for Kindle books and in CreateSpace, their print-on-demand platform for printed books.

Your description should be rich in keywords of the kind that people who would be interested in your book are likely to type into a search engine. These keywords will also be entered in the keyword section that Amazon provides further down on the product page (up to seven keywords are allowed there – but if you can think of more, you can use them in the description). The keywords should be distributed throughout the description, but ideally, the strongest keywords should appear in your first or second paragraph.

However it is important to remember that the description is not just about the quantity, it is also about the quality. Only write a long description if you have something meaningful to say about the book. You can describe the plot (not giving too much away). You can describe the issues and themes that the book addresses or touches upon. You write about the author because although Amazon offers a separate author page, you are still allowed to write about the author in the description. However make it brief. It should not replace the detailed author description you put on your Amazon author page and it should come *after* your description of the book itself.

On a related note, you can also mention other books by the same author, especially if they are on the same theme or part of the same series – e.g. "From the author of *How to solve all the world's problems from your bedroom*," or "The second in the Luscious Lesbians series."

And if you are a previously published author and this is a re-issue of a book from your back-list that you have got back from your publisher, you can quote from any published reviews that the book had elsewhere.

Categories

The category section is where you enter the category of your book, that is the genre or subject. You can in fact enter two categories and most of the categories, allow you to drill down into sub-categories. When you click on the Add Categories button, it opens up a window with a list with plus signs next to the words. Of you click on one of the categories - or the plus sign next to it - it opens up a list of sub-categories.

Most of the categories are for fiction. There is in fact only one fiction category. But if you click on it, you will find many sub-categories and these, in turn, lead to many sub-sub-categories - e.g. Fiction - Thrillers - Legal.

Choosing the right category (and keywords) is very important, because Amazon will, in the first instance, show your book to others who have bought books in the same category or with similar keywords. After you start to get sales, they will also note what other books, the people who bought your book are buying. Then they will offer your book, to more people who have bought those other books and similarly will offer those other books to people who buy your book. This is Amazon's way of serving up content to customers who are likely to be interested in it. You as a writer/publisher gain nothing from incorrectly describing your book and *everything* from describing it accurately so that it will be seen by the kind of people who are likely to be interested in it.

Keywords

Amazon allows up to seven keywords for your book. So choose carefully and make them count. As in the description, choose the kind of words of the kind that people who would be interested in your book are likely to type into a search engine. For example, if you have written a science fiction book involving space travel and laser weapons, you should make "space travel" and "laser" two of your keywords.

Remember the golden rule is to choose keywords that a potential fan of your book is likely to think of and that other authors of similar books are likely to use. This again insures that people who bought or gave positive reviews to books like yours will be shown your book by Amazon when they sign in - or even when they go to Amazon without signing in (thanks to good old cookies!).

Cover design

You have a number of options when it comes to cover design. If you have the money, and expect the book to sell well, you can pay a professional designer (you can find them via an internet search) to design your cover for you. If you have design skills, you could design a cover yourself. Or you can use the built in cover design facilities of KDP itself. These design features include a library of stock pictures you can use, or you can use one of your own pictures. Then you select from a series of options to configure and tweak the cover, to get it the way you want.

Cover image

If none of the stock pictures offered by Amazon suit you, and you don't have a suitable picture of your own, you can always buy pictures from one of the many online picture libraries that sell pictures (and the accompanying licenses) for a fee.

These fees can vary. Most picture libraries have different levels of usage and different categories of picture. I used to use ReflexStock, but then found that ShutterStock was cheaper, at least at the time. At the time of writing, one can buy the right to five images from ShutterStock for GB£32 or 25 images for GB£139. And of course, you don't have to choose or download all the images at once. Ingimage offers 10 images for GB£49.

Promoting the book

Once you have written, edited, copy-edited, proofread and published your book on the Amazon Kindle site, your work is not yet over. In fact, it has barely begun!

You now have to work your backside off *promoting* your book.

Website

One obvious way to promote your book is through a dedicated website. This can be dedicated to the book, the series (if it is part of a series) or an author website. You can get a cheap website through one of the many providers out there, with ready-made templates or you can use on of the hosted blogging platforms like WordPress, tumblr, Blogger, Medium, LiveJournal, etc. These offer a free option, but some - like WordPress - offer you more control if you pay. For example, a free WordPress site will take the form: https://thenameyouchose.wordpress.com. Whereas if you pay £15 per year, you can have https://thenameyouchose.com without "WordPress".

But of course, what really matters is how you use your website to promote the book. Obviously you can announce the book, describe it (using keywords that an interested party might type into a search engine), show the cover, write some blurb about how you came to write it. You can spice it up by showing some of the cover designs that you considered but then rejected.

You can write about yourself, your background. Then get all your friends who have websites or blogs to put in a link to your site and maybe say a few words about it.(You might have to do the same for them, but not at the same time. Leave it a week. Or put in links to their site first and blog about them.

If you have done a print version of the book, you can do a giveaway, inviting people to apply and leave their eMail addresses with one lucky winner (or a few) getting signed editions of the book. This will enable you to get eMail addresses for follow-up sales eMails both about that book and others you write in the future - or those you have written in the past for that matter.

But the main thing about a website or blog is that it should be *maintained*. Website pickup some search engine status just by being around for a long time. But if they don't change over time, this can

229

count against them. It may not completely undermine the benefit they get from their longevity, but it certainly erodes it. If you constantly add new material to your website or blog, it will not only be crawled more often by the search engines, but will also rise in rank because it will be recognized as a site that is well-maintained and fresh.

But what do you put on the site to update it so much? Even if it is a site or blog for the series or an author site for *all* your books, how can you keep it fresh and constantly updated?

Well first of all you can keep a diary of the latest book you are working on, describing your progress and troubles. This doesn't have to be once a day, but it can be once or twice a week. You can also write about other things, like fan-mail (real or imaginary), things in the news that annoyed/interested/surprised you. The important thing is that the more you update your website or blog , the more it gets crawled by the search engines and the higher it gets (and stays) in the rankings.

There is also a case for having several websites/blogs (not obviously in your name) and using these to promote your book in addition to having other uses. These can include book review blogs. You can use these to review books by other independent authors and use this to incentivize hem to review yours. Do not explicitly ask them for such a quid pro quo (unless you know them personally) as this might offend them. But you can review their book(s) positively and then write to them and mention the fact that you liked their book and reviewed it and then suggest to them that they might be interested in reading yours and would be happy to send them a free copy. They *should* be able to take the hint.

Another advantage of having multiple blogs and websites is that you can have links on all of them to the page(s) for your book(s) on Amazon. This raises your book's search engine juice.

Social Media

Use your Facebook account to tell all your friends about your book. Ask them to spread the word to *their* friends. Ask them to review it. You can do a free giveaway (see below) on Amazon and tell them to download a free copy then. This may not count as a sale but it registers as interest in your book. If they then read and review it, you will then have some reviews (see below) which will break the ice in the eyes of potential readers.

Create a Page on Facebook for your book and invite all your friends to join. Place an extract or two from the book on the book's Facebook page. Do not do this all at once: pace it and space it out. Ask your friends to spread the word to others and to invite *their* friends to join the page. But do not be disappointed if very few of them respond. Their can be a great deal of apathy among Facebook friends, whilst the close friends - the ones who are your friends in real life - all know each other and are part of the same circle, so it will be much harder to use them to extend the word to more people.

Use Twitter to tell your friends about the book. Add a link to the Amazon page for the book and ask them to click on the link and check it out.

Their are other Social Media and Social Bookmarking sites where you can register and then tag/bookmark or otherwise spread the word about the book. A single tag or bookmark may be largely ignored, but if you can persuade your friends to tag, bookmark or vote for the URL of the book's Amazon page too, that can help the page rise through the rankings. Remember that it is important to get many *different* users to tag or bookmark the URL - ideally on several different social bookmarking and social news sites.

Also - and this is very important - because a book's page at Amazon can have more than one URL, depending on how one searches for it, **make sure that you are consistent in which URL you use.**

Ideally, you should identify the simplest form of the product page's URL and use that in all social media, blogs, websites, bookmarks and tags. And make sure that your friends do so too. The form of the URL would be:

http://www.amazon.com/Your-Book-Title-Here-ebook/dp/Bxxxxxxxxx

Where each x is a letter or number.

If it is a print edition published through the CreateSpace platform, the URL will be:

http://www.amazon.com/ Your-Book-Title-Here-Volume/dp/nnnnnnnnnn

Where the n is a number.
The important social bookmarking sites are: digg, delicious, StumbleUpon, reddit, tumblr, diigo, Startaid and Pinterest.

Digg apparently counts very highly in the Google rankings and even a few votes there carry a lot of weight. **Delicious** is owned by Yahoo and similarly carries a lot of weight with them. **Reddit** is one of the big boys and should definitely not be ignored! **StumbleUpon** is owned by eBay and is another of the big boys. **Startaid** apparently ranks highly in the search engines. But remember there are many more and the sands are constantly shifting. It has also been suggested that even Google bookmarks are important because Google can keep track of them and accord greater importance and ranking status to the URLs that are bookmarked more.

Reviews

When I see a book (or other product)on Amazon and it says "Be the first to review this item," I run a mile. That may be wrong of me, but it is a natural impulse - and I am not alone. No one wants to be the guinea pig. The biggest enemy of a book is not bad reviews, but *no* reviews. Who wants to be the one who tries it first? We all want some semblance of information from some one else - especially when we have so many titles to choose from.

232

So it is *vital* that you get people to review your book, both on Amazon and any other major retail sites where it is available. There is also a case for getting it reviewed on reader sites like Goodreads and LibraryThing, as well as by independent reviewers.

Start by asking your family and friends to review it on Amazon. I have found in the past that in many cases the reply one gets is "when I get around to it." I have even suggested, in the past, that the writer should write reviews for their lazy family and friends and get them to post those reviews. I probably wouldn't advise that now. But it is important to remember that without reviews, your book will never get off the ground. Ideally they should be good reviews. But remember that while it is the five star reviews that pack the most punch in the rankings and the algorithms that push the books, it is the four star and three star reviews that are the most convincing to human readers when they weigh up the reviews. Also, sales - and even free downloads (see below) - pack more punch with the algorithms than reviews. And reviews by those who have *bought the book* or taken it a free download carry more weight than other reviews when it comes to the algorithm pushing the book.

Another thing to bear in mind is that while it is tempting to dash off a short review to save time, people are more likely to be convinced by a long review that contains useful information. Even if the product description states what the book is about, a good review can elaborate on this, bringing out the theme, the key characters and the impression that the book made on the reader. So ask your friends to write long reviews and to go into detail about *why* they like it and what it's about.

If you are really serious about getting your book reviewed, the way to do it is to get independent reviewers on board. The Indie Review list http://www.theindieview.com/indie-reviewers/ publishes a list of 299 book review sites (at the latest count) that review books *without charging money*. An internet search for "Book review sites" will almost certainly reveal other lists of sites not listed by the Indie Review site. Look for reviewers who are interested in reviewing your genre/type of book and send it to them or fill out their submission form. Make sure you read their rules and submission procedures and follow them scrupulously.

But watch out for "bait and switch" scams - where they say on the site that they do free reviews but then when you write to them, they try to charge you money.

The good thing about these independent reviewers is that they post their reviews on multiple platforms. This typically means their own website, Amazon, Goodreads and sometimes LibraryThing.

Amazon Giveaways

If you enroll your book under KDP Select for 90 days, you can then give it away free for up to five days within that 90 day period. However, this requires that you sell the eBook edition of the book *exclusively* on the Kindle for that 90 day period. You must also own world rights to the book in order to do this - even if you yourself choose not to sell it worldwide.

Also be careful when enrolling it to make sure that the button by "Automatically renew this book's enrollment in KDP Select for another 90 days." is unchecked, otherwise it will automatically roll over the enrollment for another 90 days, when the first 90 days runs out. This button used to be checked by default, but I am not sure whether that is still the case now. At any rate, you can uncheck the button any time within the 90 days until it actually *does* roll over. But it is better to keep the button unchecked. That puts you in control.

You might think that such a giveaway, simply represents a loss of sales. But I did a five day giveaway on my legal thriller Mercy and after five days in which 15000 free copies were downloaded, *sales went through the roof!* It also got loads of reviews after that -most of them positive - which further boosted sales.

Goodreads Giveaways

You can also do Giveaways on Goodreads. In this case, it is for print copies of the book (e.g. copies that you print on demand via CreateSpace). Also, in this case, instead of giving it away to all comers, you hold a contest designating a limited number of winners. Goodreads will host the contest, letting people apply until the deadline you set and then at the end, they will randomly select the winners and notify you of who they are so that you can send them the copies.

The purpose of a Goodreads giveaway is to get reviews and many recipients do indeed write such reviews and you can request that they do so. But they are under no *obligation* to review your book. And even if they choose to review it, they are under no obligation to give it a *positive* review.

To do a Goodreads giveaway, you must first register as an author with Goodreads. This will give you an author account with an Author Dashboard and access to the Author tools. To do a giveaway, you go to the book's page on Goodreads (not your Author Dashboard). In the top right corner you will see rectangle with curved corners where it says "Author Tools" and just below that three item in green:

Book stats | Widget | List a giveaway

Select "List a giveaway" and this will take you to the giveaway page where you enter the details of the giveaway you are planning. These items include:-

- the start and end dates of the giveaway

- the book release date (which can be before or after the start or end of the giveaway - i.e. you can do a pre-release giveaway *or* a post-release giveaway)

- the book ID or ISBN (the ID is an internal number generated by Goodreads and is entered by default when you go to the page

235

- the "Eligible Countries" for the release from a scroll down list - you can limit it to certain countries or do multiple giveaways, designating different countries and different numbers of copies A checkbox for whether or not the book contains "mature content"

- A description of the book giveaway in your own words (up to 1500 characters)

- The prime genre of the book from a drop-down list

- A secondary genre of the book (optional) from the same drop-down list

- Your contact information.

After you have entered all this information and clicked on the check box at the bottom confirming that you agree to the terms and conditions set by Goodreads, you click on save and the giveaway as started.

While the giveaway is in progress you will be able to monitor its progress from your Author Dashboard. Scroll down to the bottom of your Dashboard and you will see a section marked "Your Giveaways". This will show your most recent giveaways. You can also click on the link marked "All of Your giveaways" - this will take you to a new page showing all of your giveaways (past and present) and not just the most recent. This will show you how many people requested or are requesting your book - i.e. how many people have signed up for the giveaway. Remember the more people who ask for your book, the more interest there is in the book!

To see how your giveaway is doing compared to others, click on the down arrow next to the word "Explore" at the top of every Goodreads page. This will open a drop down list. The third item on this list is "Giveaways". Click on this word and it will take you to a page that shows the giveaways in progress. This page has four tabs near the top, but not at the top.

The first tab - selected by default - is "Ending Soon". This shows the giveaways that have an ending date that is coming up in the near future. On the left it shows the cover, then the name of the book. And on the right it shows the time that the giveaway ends, how many copies are offered (i.e. how many people will get free copies), how many are currently requesting the book (a measure of how popular it is), the start and end dates of the giveaway and the countries (or rather two letter country codes) where people are eligible to apply.

These variables are all set by you. The reason you can specify the country is two-fold. First of all, in some cases you might not have the right to giveaway the book in all countries (e.g. if you have sold it to some publishers in some countries). Secondly, it is expensive to send books to some countries and you might wish to keep down your costs.

The second tab shows the "Most Requested" books. In effect this is a chart of the leaders in terms of popularity. If you get into a high position on this list, it means that your book has aroused a lot of interest. Unlike an Amazon Kindle giveaway to all-comers, this doesn't mean that you're actually giving away a lot of free copies. The number that you giveaway is set by you at the beginning. What it means is that a lot of people *want* your book and are trying their best to get it free. But they may very well be ready to pay if the Goodreads algorithm doesn't choose them as the recipient, or one of the recipients, of a free copy.

The third tab shows giveaways by popular (i.e. major) authors. These are usually arranged by the publishers. A quick glance at the current crop shows that they fare no better than their less well-known counterparts. Thus a book by Dean Koontz with 50 copies available, tops the list with 336 people requesting. Admittedly this is only four days into a 17 day giveaway. But on the other hand, the book in third position on the first tab is ten days into a 20 day giveaway, and yet is has 5359 people requesting it and only *one copy available!*

The forth tab show recently listed giveaways. Topping the list is an eight day giveaway that already has 199 applicants for one copy - and it only started today!

Clearly then, Goodreads giveaways are an excellent way to promote your book and create internet buzz.

Other giveaways, cover reveals, guest posts, interviews, blog tours, etc.

When you send out your book to independent reviewers, you can also do cover reveals, interviews and blog tours. Cover reveals are self-explanatory, but only worthwhile if done *before* publication. Interviews are done as written questions which you answer in writing and send back by eMail. Sometimes the questions are fixed, other times they offer you a lot of questions but ask you to pick a few.

Blog tours are virtual tours in which you go from blog to blog, as if you were going from place to place. The tour "stops" (which you arrange in advance with the various bloggers) consist of interviews, reviews and guest/promotional posts that the bloggers let you submit to their blogs for publication on the agreed date. There are blog tour companies, who arrange these blog tours, for a fee. Or you can organize your own. Generally speaking you would cover between 20 and 60 blogs on a tour, contacting the blog owners in advance and arranging it with them - if you are doing it yourself. Once the dates are agreed with the blog owner, you would write the guest posts, answer the interview questions and submit the book for review about three weeks in advance, to give the blog owners time to do their bit.

If you are doing the publicity yourself, check out the Indie Review list and the websites of its 300 listed reviewers. Many of them offer one or more of these options. Remember, they are looking for content for their websites. You are giving them content and in return they are giving you publicity. Approach them politely and you can get a lot back from them.

A final word

So we end up here the end of my book but hopefully at the beginning of yours. This book should give you the tools - and the confidence - to set about the task of becoming a successful Amazon Kindle author. Remember that although everything written here is based on this author's experience, nothing in this book is written in stone. (It is after all an e-Book.)

So take what you can from this book - whatever ideas you choose - but feel free to disagree with me on any and every matter. To be a writer, you must first be a thinker. Listen to others, but think for yourselves. In the words of that famous *Monty Python* movie: "You are all individuals!"

And if you liked this book and found it interesting and informative, please don't forget to review it, at minimum on Amazon. And also, if you have the time, review it on Goodreads and/or LibraryThing, your own blog or website (with a link to the book's page on Amazon) and also in other social media like Facebook, Twitter, Reddit, Digg, Tumblr, Delicious, StumbleUpon, etc - again with a link to the book's page at Amazon.

And now, sit down at your word processor with a cup of coffee, roll up your sleeves (without spilling the coffee all over your keyboard) and write that bestseller than you know you have in you!

THE END

www.ingramcontent.com/pod-product-compliance
Lightning Source LLC
Chambersburg PA
CBHW071338280526
45787CB00001B/138